Paul—A Jew on the Margins

PAUL—A JEW
ON THE MARGINS

Calvin J. Roetzel

Westminster John Knox Press
LOUISVILLE • LONDON

Scripture quotations from the New Revised Standard Version of the Bible are copyright © 1989 by the Division of Christian Education of the National Council of the Churches of Christ in the U.S.A. and are used by permission.

Chapter 3 in revised form is published in *Common Life in the Early Church, Essays Honoring Graydon F. Snyder,* ed. Julian V. Hills (Harrisburg, Pa.: Trinity Press International, 1998), and is used here by permission.

Chapter 4 in revised form is published in *Interpretation, A Journal of Bible and Theology* 46/1 (1992), and is used here by permission.

Chapter 5 in revised form is published in *Diaspora Jews and Judaism, Essays in Honor of, and in Dialogue with, A. Thomas Kraabel,* ed. J. Andrew Overman and Robert S. MacLennan (Atlanta: Scholars Press, 1992), and is used here by permission.

Chapter 6 in revised form is published in *Pauline Theology, Volume II,* ed. David M. Hay (Minneapolis: Fortress Press, 1993), and is used here by permission.

Book design by Sharon Adams
Cover design by Mark Abrams

On the cover is a depiction of Saint Paul, a detail from the *Sant' Emidio* by Carlo Crivelli.

First edition
Published by Westminster John Knox Press
Louisville, Kentucky

This book is printed on acid-free paper that meets the American National Standards Institute Z39.48 standard. ♾

PRINTED IN THE UNITED STATES OF AMERICA

03 04 05 06 07 08 09 10 11 12 — 10 9 8 7 6 5 4 3 2 1

Library of Congress Cataloging-in-Publication Data is on file at the Library of Congress, Washington, D.C.

ISBN 0-664-22520-9

In honor of Wanda
and in memory of Franklin, Leonard, and Lavon

Contents

Preface

Over the years I have come to see Paul more and more as a marginal Jew who stood on the boundary between religious convictions and cultural commitments that strained in opposite directions. Some have thought of Paul as a divided person, with one foot in his Jewish cultural homeland and the other in an urban Hellenistic setting, but a citizen of neither. Still others persist in their imaging of Paul as a "former Jew" who after his encounter with Christ became an apostate from Judaism, "converting" to Christianity. Increasingly, I am drawn to the opposite position, as I have noted elsewhere: "that Paul did not just *use* Hellenistic language, anthropology, and worldviews as mute, value-neutral entities but that he was influenced by them at a deep level."[1] Though I would agree that Paul did radically revise his understanding of Israel's story and its scriptures in light of his encounter with Christ, the view of Paul as an apostate is a post facto creation that is anachronistic. I am persuaded by Daniel Boyarin that the great and ugly divorce between Judaism and Christianity came much later.[2] Paul's mission to the *ethnē* (Gentiles) generated sharp and explosive tensions between him and the Jerusalem church, between him and some synagogues, and between him and rival apostles alive with a vision of Christ at odds with his own.

I use the term *marginal* throughout these essays in a sense at odds with that used in some circles. Although I appreciate the value of recognizing the marginality of the dislocated poor in an urban shantytown, I use the word somewhat differently in Paul's case. As I note in chapter 1, I apply the term to Paul to describe his cultural and religious alienation, the special place on the margin of the ages that he occupies by divine call, and the location that offers an opportunity for radical openness. Given the diversity in the early Jesus movement and the Judaism(s) of Paul's day, I readily recognize the impossibility of drawing a margin from one nucleus, for there was no one margin to serve as the compass point. Yet, as I note later, I am convinced that in different degrees Paul experienced alienation from a number of religious combines.

I was encouraged by Carey Newman to bring together a series of essays that have appeared in some venues that may not be readily accessible. In looking at the essays, I was surprised to learn that for a number of years I had been dealing with issues related to Paul's life on the margin. Some were excluded because they did not readily adapt to the others of this collection. All of the chapters except for the first and second have appeared in penultimate form in print elsewhere. I am especially grateful to the staff and editors of Westminster John Knox Press for their patience with my plodding pace. Greg Glover has encouraged this project since he joined Westminster John Knox Press. Daniel Braden has skillfully and sensitively directed the manuscript through each publication phase. His suggestions have been invaluable. Don Parker-Burgard, who edited the copy, did an exemplary job. Since I first came to Macalester College in 1969, I have always received generous support for my research and writing projects. I am especially grateful to Toni Schrantz, our able office assistant, who cheerfully and ably assisted with many of the daily chores associated with getting a manuscript to a publisher. It was she who enlisted Sarah Chamberlain and Amber Converse to scan copies and correct previously published essays into a readable form. And both Sarah and Amber were wonderful—diligent, careful, and enthusiastic about being involved in this project.

My debt to many, named and nameless, is profound, and this volume owes much to them all. Here, however, I must pay tribute to the family of my youth, especially to my brothers and my sister. My brother and first teacher, Lavon, told me my first nursery rhymes and fairy tales, taught me my first songs, my ABCs, and often ushered me into a magical story world. My sister and soul mate, Wanda, was my constant companion and playmate in my childhood, and my constant source of support and encouragement in my adult years. It is no accident that we both became teachers. My oldest brother, Franklin, was like a second father to me. He bought me my first bicycle and my first leather jacket when times were hard. He loaned me his car for dates, and he did yeoman's service when my parents were old. He went on to become a public servant who gave himself generously to a number of important causes. His memory is fresh and rich. My brother Leonard was a strong and generous model; he loved the ocean and found a way to laugh even in life's low tides. His strength, generosity, and good humor brought joy to many, and the memory of them still brightens my days. In different and important ways this book belongs to them all.

Abbreviations

WBC	Word Biblical Commentary
ZAW	*Zeitschrift für die altestamentliche Wissenschaft*
ZNW	*Zeitschrift für die neutestamentliche Wissenschaft und die Kunde der älteren Kirche*
ZTK	*Zeitschrift für Theologie und Kirche*

Chapter 1

Paul—A Jew on the Margins

In her autobiographical essay "Choosing the Margin as a Space of Radical Openness," bell hooks recalls the pain of her early years in a segregated southern town in Kentucky. From that shantytown with its dirt streets and boarded-up houses she looked across the tracks at a city with paved streets, stores she could not enter, restaurants she could not dine in, and theaters whose main floors were closed to African Americans. She recalls that her people could enter that white world only temporarily to work as janitors, or maids, or prostitutes, or nannies, or gardeners, or street sweepers. They could not live there. "We could enter that world," she notes, but "we had always to return to the margin."[1]

As a young woman, bell hooks left that world for a university where she could live in open housing, could see independent cinema, read critical theory, write critical theory, and eventually assume a post where she could carve out a space as a university professor. She speaks poignantly of the marginalization, alienation, and estrangement she felt in both worlds. Yet she distinguishes between the different types of marginality—one imposed by oppressive forces from without and the other somewhat more ambiguous but, nevertheless, real. From her experience of living on the margin she has made an astounding discovery of the margin as awful and dehumanizing but also as a place of "radical openness and possibility."[2] Thus, she distinguishes between two types of marginality—one assigned, and the other embraced. The marginality she owns offers new ways of constructing reality and frontiers of difference.[3] From that margin she has not only constructed a world of possibility but she views her home as center in a totally different way, and from that center she views the margin as a space pregnant with possibility. From one has come a strong sense of self and communal solidarity. From the other has come a vision of a new creation.

Assigning individuals or groups to marginal status is a willful political act normally used to maintain the status quo and to serve the interests of those with the power to make such an assignment. It is damaging, dehumanizing, and demeaning. In such cases, those who are powerful locate themselves at the center and attempt to push those who are deemed threatening to the margin. Those in power, however, hardly have the last word. Even the powerless have power—power bestowed by their imagination, their language, their spirit, and their deep convictions. Through their imaginative constructions, their visions of a new world, their defiant assertion of their worth through the creative process, they accept their marginality as an opportunity for radical possibility. In one case the marginality is assigned, in the other case the marginality is owned and creatively exploited.

Paul, who saw himself as an apocalyptic messenger with an apocalyptic message, clearly fits both categories. He indeed felt chosen to serve on a cosmic margin drawn by the God of Israel in Christ. The conviction that a new age was dawning and the old eon was passing away governed his activity. He was sure that he was living on the cusp of an eschatological breakthrough that would come to fruition in his lifetime. The enormous anticipation, optimism, and energy this understanding provided is difficult to overestimate. This divine placement on the margin established Paul as a liminal figure who creatively embraced this location even though it was fraught with peril, suffused with ambiguity, and complicated by the mingling of competing forces. Moreover, because of the urgency of the times, he accepted this placement as a locus of radical possibility. Paul saw in this incandescent moment the prospect of reconciling an alien world to its Creator, and reconciling the "outsiders" to the "insiders."

While there is an ocean of difference between Paul, a first-century Mediterranean Jew, and bell hooks, an African American woman from the American South, they share an experience of marginality. Paul, of course, hardly saw himself as a member of the underclass, and the margin to which he was assigned had nothing whatever to do with race. In some ways, he was among the elite. He was highly literate, he knew and used Hellenistic literary conventions, he was aware of Stoic philosophy and Hellenistic rhetoric, he was steeped in the Jewish tradition and knew and used sophisticated hermeneutical methods, and he was fully at home in the Greek language. All of these assured him a place of privilege. Yet his acceptance of Jesus as the Jewish Messiah, his claim to be an apostle of that Jesus, and his version of the gospel that included the Gentiles in God's covenant people placed him at odds with both non-Christian Jews and Jewish Christians in Jerusalem. Moreover, his invitation to Gentiles to become a part of the elect of the God of Israel brought the ire of powerful religio-cultural forces that were enormously threatened by Paul's strategy. The representatives of these religio-cultural forces acted to minimize Paul's influence by assigning Paul a marginal status.

I am acutely aware of the risks of calling Paul a marginal Jew. Marginality suggests a center from which a periphery can be drawn. It is a truism that in the first century there was neither a normative Judaism nor an orthodox Christianity that formed a nucleus from which one could draw a circumference. There were multiple expressions of each. However, the Jerusalem church—through its direct historical connections to Jesus through the disciples Peter, James, and John, and through Jesus' brother James—enjoyed an influence and authority that was dominant throughout Paul's life as an apostle. It saw Paul's radical protocol for including Gentiles among God's elect without precondition or benefit of the usual law observance that marked entrance into the family of God as provocative and even an outrageous novelty. Paul's letter to the Galatians well documents the tensions between him and Peter, James, and the so-called pillars of the Jerusalem church. Paul's casual attitude toward matters of ritual purity and law observance inevitably placed him at odds with Pharisaism. And his indifference or even hostility to the apostolic marks of charismatic power among roving Hellenistic Jewish apostles further alienated him. Many groups who considered themselves privileged in some sense located Paul far to the side of their main concerns. Pressures to locate Paul on the margin came from many different hubs of power.

I suggest that Paul's marginal status, like that of bell hooks, however, was more than one imposed by a religio-political power center. Paul actively embraced the margin and made it an instrument pregnant with possibility. We may be in a better position to understand some of the forces inspiring bell hooks's embrace of the margin as a site of radical possibility than with those that inspired Paul. We know the nature of segregation in America and we understand in part the enormous harm it did to human life. We can still see remnants of it embedded in our society. Alternatively, we have no firsthand knowledge of the alienation Paul experienced. Yet we do gain from his undisputed letters some insight into the pressures to which Paul was subjected and the way he turned that assigned location of marginality into a stinging rebuke of his critics and into a soaring affirmation of his gospel.

In my discussion of Paul's marginal status, I go beyond John Meier, who appropriates a sociological application of the word *marginal* to refer to poor migrants who resist integration into an urban culture. Drawing on the work of Janice Perlman, Meier has characterized Jesus as a poor, uncredentialed Galilean layman who clashed with the rich, powerful, privileged, aristocratic Jerusalem priesthood, and so disturbed the religious and political establishment and so provoked them that they participated in his rejection and crucifixion.[4] Meier thus finds in the adjective *marginal* the key for understanding Jesus' ministry and prophetic activity.[5]

Paul, on the other hand, shared few of these traits with Jesus. He was an urban, not a rural, figure. He was a diaspora Jew rather than a Palestinian Jew. Though both Paul and Jesus had an itinerant ministry, the teaching style of the Jesus of the Gospels and that of Paul of the Epistles were worlds apart. In the Gospels, Jesus teaches in parables; in the Epistles, Paul weaves long complicated arguments and refers to none of Jesus' parables. In the Gospels, Jesus proclaims the kingdom of God; in the Epistles, Paul pays scant attention to the kingdom. Of course, Jesus is hailed as the Messiah, and Paul as an apostle of the Messiah. And whereas the Jesus of the Gospels is clearly presented as a marginal figure, we have nothing from Jesus himself that would reveal his own understanding of that issue. Paul not only recognized his marginal status, but he embraced it as a venue of dramatic, even revolutionary, possibility.

In the ancient world as in our own, the precise location of the margin is often unclear. Similarly, when bell hooks enrolled in a university in the North, the precise line of separation was less clear and its message more ambiguous than in the southern town of her youth. In the university, marginality was often a matter of degrees, but no less real.

Paul's life on the margin as an apostle of Christ was also fraught with ambiguity, and that ambiguity has fostered wildly different interpretations of its meaning. Looking at parts of the letters, some scholars are convinced that Paul was an apostate from Judaism and thus not on the margin of Judaism but outside it altogether. They see in passages such as Galatians 4:21–31 and Philippians 3:4–11 a warrant for calling Paul a "former Jew" who renounced his home in favor of a distant, alien land. For these scholars, Paul's prior life becomes almost totally inessential, as "dark background and as harshly drawn contrast to the beginning of his second, real life."[6] Over a century ago, Adolf von Harnack insisted that Paul had "delivered the Christian religion from Judaism."[7] His contemporary Wilhelm Wrede similarly thought Paul understood faith as no longer *Jewish* but as a new faith. Contemporary scholars such as Alan Segal, Ed Sanders, Tom Wright, and Hyam Maccoby, though very different from each other, all emphasize the discontinuity between Paul and his native Judaism.

Side by side with those passages from Galatians and Philippians, however, one can find other passages in which Paul affirms his native religion. Without question, the God he addressed was the God of Israel. His scriptures were the holy writings of Israel, and nowhere did he let go of Torah as God's word, though he certainly did reinterpret it.[8] His Christ, as the Messiah, is Davidic. His forefather according to the flesh is Abraham; his foremother is Sarah. The prophets in whom he finds allusions to the Messiah are the prophets of Israel. His eschatology was Jewish through and through, and his Pharisaism was obviously a zealous form of Judaism. Second Corinthians, from rather late in Paul's apostolic career, answers the fierce rivals who question the authenticity of Paul's apostleship. "Are they Hebrews?" he asks. "So *am* I," he adds. "Are they Israelites? So *am* I." "Are they descendants of Abraham? So am I," he counters. "Are they ministers of Christ? I am talking like a madman—I am a better one," he argues (2 Cor.

11:22–23, emphasis added). In Romans, his last letter, Paul speaks autobiographically: "I myself am an Israelite, a descendant of Abraham, a member of the tribe of Benjamin" (Rom. 11:1).

These apparent discrepancies reflect more the ambiguity of living on the margin than they reveal actual contradictions, and are due in large part to the tension between boundlessness and boundedness.[9] By examining the points of friction between Paul and those who sought to marginalize him, we gain some sense of the issues for which he fought and how his theology developed as he was engaged in this interactive process. Paul believed his moment in history was a time of radical, dramatic, revolutionary, convulsive change, and that an apocalyptic breakthrough was inaugurated in the death and resurrection of Jesus. The theological implications of that epiphany came gradually in the thick of the fray over the validity of his gospel, his call, and his apostleship.[10] The unfolding of Paul's thinking about election, surely one of the core convictions of Paul's native Judaism, illustrates this process. It was Paul's adaptation of this conviction that was most fiercely contested by the Jerusalem church, rival apostles, and non-Christian Jews.

Paul wrote 1 Thessalonians, the first letter we have from his hand, some weeks after his ministry in Thessalonica was cut short by local opposition. The apostle was in so much anguish about the church he left behind that he dispatched Timothy by foot from Athens to "strengthen and encourage" his converts in Thessalonica (3:1–2). Timothy returned some weeks later to report that great affection remained for Paul but that it was mingled with deep suspicions. Some wondered if Paul was just another popular philosopher who breezed into town, wowed a circle of admirers, lined his own pockets, and then skipped out when opposition developed. Serious problems remained. Persecution threatened to lead to the defection of some converts, the premature death of some converts who expected to be alive to welcome the returning Jesus had produced a crisis, and the idleness of some had imposed a hardship on others.

To these converts bereft of their native religion, extended family, friends, jobs, and social location, and who now faced physical and psychological abuse, Paul offers a language of inclusion, consolation, and encouragement. With the traditional language of their place among God's elect (1:4), Paul weaves a rich texture of family metaphors. He refers to his converts as the chosen of God, the elect (1:4); later he notes that they are destined for salvation (5:9). He names God as father, the converts as God's beloved children, and all converts as brothers and sisters (nineteen times in five short chapters). And this vision of an inclusive family was set in an eschatological narrative frame that set Jesus the Christ at the beginning and looked forward to his return.

While Norman Peterson has argued that these kinship metaphors were primary for Paul and therefore more important than the concept of election, there is no need to choose one over the other. For Paul, the household is constitutive of the end-time elect, and the elect are constituted as God's family. The metaphors interact, and each enriches the other. What is surprising is Paul's inclusion of Gentiles *as* Gentiles in the family of God, or among the elect, without any reference to Jewish boundary markers—circumcision, and the observance of the laws of purity, festivals, and Sabbath observance. And he does so without a single citation of the Hebrew Bible and with no reference whatever to Israel's election or its sacred story. It seems that Paul had simply not thought through the implications of his proclamation, or perhaps there was no incentive to do so. His announcement of the inclusion of Gentile converts—whom many judged as irrational, chaotic, immoral, pagan, "other"—was an expression of eschatological hope that in the last days non-Jews would honor Israel's God and be included among the chosen.

The great debate that began in Galatians about a gospel that embraced Gentile believers without law observance as a precondition for inclusion in God's elect finally ended in Romans. Paul stood, he believed, on the boundary of two worlds—one dying and one being born. He believed the dawning new age fundamentally altered the terms of inclusion in the family of God. Without precondition the Gentiles were welcomed by faith into the people of God. While Paul was aware of disturbances in Philippi set loose by Jewish Christian rivals, it was the challenge of Judaizing teachers in Galatia that triggered his most vigorous defense of accepting Gentiles *qua* Gentiles into God's elect. Appealing to Scripture and tradition, his antagonists excoriated Paul for this dangerous innovation. In response, Paul recalled his nose-to-nose confrontation with Peter in Antioch.

He accused Peter of hypocrisy for eating and consorting with pagan converts at first but drawing back when "those of the circumcision" and "those of James" from Jerusalem arrived. Paul's snarling description of Peter's duplicity reveals Paul's location on the margin, and the harshness of his rhetoric reveals how desperate he was to defend both his apostleship and his gospel. Paul's painful memory of that assault on his apostolic legitimacy suggests that Paul did not win the struggle in Antioch. Even Barnabas, his trusted fellow missionary to the Gentiles, and "the rest of the Jews" went over to the opposition (Gal. 2:13). He can hardly recall the endorsement of his Gentile gospel by the Jerusalem leaders without a caustic aside, referring to James, Cephas, and John as "reputed" pillars (Gal. 2:9, RSV, emphasis mine).

The sting from that angry encounter lingers to inform the argument here. Over a century later the *Kerygmata Petrou* has Peter condemn Paul as a false prophet, an impostor preaching a false gospel (H II 17.3), the "feeble left hand [of God, i.e., the evil one]" (H II 15.5). Contrasted with Peter, Paul appears as darkness as opposed to light, as ignorance to knowledge, as sickness to health. He is called a liar making "preposterous" and even "demonic" claims (H II 15.5; 17.3). Seeking to discredit Paul's appeal to an epiphany of Christ to legitimize his apostleship, Peter says:

> We know . . . that many idolaters, adulterers and other sinners have seen visions and had true dreams, and also that some have had visions that were wrought by demons. . . . But if you were visited by him [Christ] for the space

of an hour and were instructed by him and thereby have become an apostle, then proclaim his words, expound what he has taught, be a friend to his apostles and do not contend with me, who am his confidant; for you have in hostility withstood me, who am a firm rock, the foundation stone of the church. (H XVII 19.1–4)[11] (H II 16.1, 19.4)

While this slashing attack on Paul comes from the second century, it did represent an important view of the apostle that may in fact have been shared by first-century communities with the power to marginalize Paul.

ON THE MARGIN OF PHARISAISM

In Philippians 3:4–8, Paul shares a rare piece of his religious autobiography:

> If anyone else has reason to be confident in the flesh, I have more: circumcised on the eighth day, a member of the people of Israel, of the tribe of Benjamin, a Hebrew born of Hebrews; as to the law, a Pharisee [kata nomon pharisaios]; as to zeal, a persecutor of the church; as to righteousness under the law, blameless. Yet whatever gains I had, these I have come to regard as loss because of Christ. More than that, I regard everything as loss because of the surpassing value of knowing Christ Jesus my Lord.

While Luke's portrait of Paul in Acts underscores and affirms Paul's Pharisaism (22:3; 23:6; 26:4), only here in the letters does Paul explicitly associate himself with the Pharisees. Whether he was a devoted Pharisee or merely sympathetic to the Pharisaic interpretation of the law, we can hardly know.[12] The source of this preference is hidden from us. Did it come from his parents as Acts 23:6 alleges, or from the tutelage of Gamaliel II in Jerusalem (Acts 22:3), or simply from a vibrant, liberal Jewish community in Tarsus? We cannot know with certainty. In any case, the Epistles do reveal an affinity for and vestiges of a Pharisaic inclination.[13] His appeal to a broad scriptural tradition, his spiritualization of the sacrificial cult (e.g., Rom. 12:1; 15:18), and of course his ready owning of the resurrection of Jesus as the "first fruits of those who have fallen asleep" all point to Pharisaic influence if not lineage.

As I wondered in *Paul: The Man and the Myth*, the holiness language that suffused Paul's letters seems to hint at a Pharisaic link.[14] Paul's appeal to holiness to ensure blamelessness in the grand assize (1 Thess. 3:1), to purge the community of the "holy ones" of all impurity (1 Cor. 5:1–8), and to confirm the tie of a holy God to a holy people under orders to "be holy" are consistent with a Pharisaic genesis even if they do not require one. Nevertheless, Paul's stubborn insistence that the eschatological people of God welcome the *ethnē* (Gentiles) without precondition or the usual ritualistic markers of the elect might have struck a strict Pharisee as dangerous. Since we have no Pharisaic witness offering a rejoinder to Paul, what I here suggest is necessarily speculative. Nevertheless, this supposition would be consistent with what we know about first-century Pharisaism. Paul's place on the margin, when energized by a luminous and cosmic eschatological reality, became a locus for a breathtaking innovation.

We hardly know to what extent this apocalyptic vision had Pharisaic roots. In 70 C.E. the fall of Jerusalem, the burning of the temple, and the horrific loss of life raised the theodicy question in the sharpest possible way. How could one any longer subscribe to a feverish apocalyptic vision that promised God's intervention on behalf of the beloved city and the covenant people? Since the revolt against Roman rule was inspired in part by an apocalyptic passion, the fall of the city and the utter defeat of the revolutionary forces did much to discredit apocalypticism. By default, the Jesus people became the custodians of a rather robust collection of Jewish apocalyptic materials that fell into disfavor in many Jewish circles. The situation then, in Paul's day before the revolt, differed in some important ways from that of the postwar period. Paul was the heir to a rich and varied Jewish apocalyptic legacy, and in chapter 3 I explore the tensions that are deeply embedded in Paul's apocalyptic gospel. Paul's modification of the apocalyptic myth was so significant that many scholars understand Paul to have rejected the myth entirely. But Paul, I suggest, did not reject the myth. Rather, he reshaped it in a dramatic, revolutionary way, taking advantage of his marginal location to explore the possibilities lurking in the myth.

In the chapters that follow, it will be obvious that there are different kinds of marginality—cultural, religious, social, and even political. Moreover, following Janice Perlman, I show that marginality is a matter "of degree rather than absolutes."[15] While Paul may be marginal in some ways, and also marginal with regard to some institutions, groups, and ideologies, he may be less so with others.

In the following chapters, I draw on Perlman, who argues that the attribution of marginality can be used by those in power to suppress difference and even to secure their own interests. The attribution of marginality can also be used to preserve the status quo and to defend against political or religious challenges to nationalism, the upper class, or those in power. It can also be used to discredit threatening ideological options as wrong or even evil. The example and courageous spirit of Perlman's poor, migrant grandparents inspired her attempt to expose the fact that the invocation of marginality can be exploited to support "personal beliefs and social interests," and to provide defense so strong that it will "remain unshaken by any theoretical criticism."[16] Perlman is acutely aware of the use of marginality as a weapon of power, as is bell hooks.[17] However, hooks sketches more clearly how marginality can be embraced by the marginalized as an instrument "of radical openness and possibility."[18] In the chapters that follow, I show how Paul too saw himself as a liminal figure and responded to his location with imagination and creativity, and how this response presumed a radical reevaluation of Paul's native religion, though it in no way repudiated that faith.

Chapter 2

Paul as Mother

A Metaphor for Jewish-Christian Conversion?

We must face the issue of conversion immediately, because if Paul were a convert—that is, if Paul had left one religion for another—then any discussion of his marginal status as a Jew would be largely superfluous. Relying on the seminal work of Caroline Walker Bynum, I offer an alternative understanding of Paul's "conversion." Some attention to the underlying issues concerning this topic is therefore necessary.

The Oxford English Dictionary offers sixteen different definitions of *conversion*. The preferred definition deals with a change of religion: "The bringing of anyone over to a specified religious faith, profession, or party, esp. to one regarded as true, from what is regarded as falsehood or error. (Without qualification, usually = conversion to Christianity)." I want to begin with a consideration of the apostle Paul, who was in the early centuries the prototype of conversion. He is an important figure not only because there is a large corpus of secondary literature that deals with his so-called conversion, but also because the way this issue has been resolved profoundly affects the way all of the Pauline Epistles have been read throughout the centuries, and even how the Acts of the Apostles has been and continues to be understood.

CONVERSION: REJECTION OF
ONE RELIGION FOR ANOTHER

There is not much in the Bible about conversion. The word itself does not appear, though there are words that suggest dramatic change, such as *shub* in Hebrew and *epistrephō* or *epistrepsate* in Greek. In his classic study *Conversion*, first articulated in the Donnellan Lectures at Trinity College, Dublin, Arthur Darby Nock sought to place the phenomenon of conversion in the Hellenistic setting where early Christianity enjoyed its greatest success. In that context, Nock held that conversion was "the reorientation of the soul of an individual, his deliberate turning from indifference or from an earlier form of piety to another, a turning which implies a consciousness that a great change is involved, that *the old was wrong and the new is right.*"[1] Then he added, "We cannot understand the success of Christianity outside Judaea without making an effort to determine the elements in the mind of the time to which it appealed."[2] To the extent that it was applied to Paul's own experience, Nock's work, perhaps against his wishes, provided support for those who saw an early divorce of Christianity from Pharisaic Judaism and the early development of Christianity as an autonomous and rival form of piety. Some therefore concluded that Paul's surrender to Christ represented a conversion from one religion to another. Christianity and Judaism thus were cast as mutually exclusive opposites, which confronted each other in a sometimes violent manner.

There is a sense in which Nock was correct. Certainly Paul refers to those who had made just such a change. The change from the worship of "idols" to serving the "living and true God" might very aptly be called a conversion, though Paul himself nowhere uses that term. Instead, Paul prefers "turning" (*epestrepsate*; 1 Thess. 1:9), or he contrasts the former time "when you did not know God, you were enslaved to beings that by nature are not gods" with the present eschatological moment when "you have come to know God, or rather to be known by God" (Gal. 4:8–9). He also speaks of entry into the community as a response to God's call (1 Cor. 1:26–31). This Gentile "conversion" was a sine qua non for the success of Paul's mission. It is implied also by Galatians 1:4, where Paul speaks of God's deliverance of the Galatian addressees from the "present evil age." Certainly Nock's view of conversion in the Hellenistic world is an entirely apt description of the Gentile experience of Paul's church. But Nock refused to view Paul as a convert from Judaism to Christianity, and thus avoided a serious distortion of the whole of Pauline theology. Generally, others have not been so cautious.

In his influential book *Paul, Apostle to the Gentiles* (1993), Jürgen Becker offers an understanding of conversion that applies to Paul what Nock applied to Gentiles. Becker makes Paul's call synonymous with his conversion, a transformation so radical that it separated him from his native Judaism. Becker equates Paul's apostolic call—which turned him from being an adversary to being an advocate for the Jesus movement—with conversion.[3] He traces Paul's rejection of the religion of Israel to this event:

> Paul knew—namely, in an eternally valid now—that with his calling *everything* had changed for him from now on and for all time. He himself had become someone else, and with him his entire experience of reality and his interpretation of world history. It is not by chance that we see in all the texts how Paul *discards the old* and grasps the new as his true future.[4]

As Becker puts it, Paul recognized that "he previously did all things wrong and should begin anew under completely different conditions."[5] He refers to Paul as the "*former* Jew," the "*former* Pharisee," and as an apostate from Judaism (emphasis added). He splits Paul's life into two halves that are largely discontinuous—one Jewish, the other Christian. The call, or conversion, marks the great divide between them, and leads the "Christian" Paul to dispose of his Jewish past almost entirely:

> He experienced his calling as such a profound reorientation and identity crisis that the previous part of his life becomes almost totally inessential and the time after his calling comprises his real life. Therefore in Paul's letters the Jewish portion of his life is not presented at all for its own sake. It only serves here and there, sporadically and typified by a few narrowly limited statements, as *dark background and as harshly drawn contrast* to the beginning of his second, real life.[6]

The call of Paul, Becker notes, displayed no continuity with the call of the prophets Jeremiah and Isaiah who, like Paul, understood themselves to have been set aside from their mothers' wombs. His experience was more like a conversion that disassociated Paul from his Jewish past.

Paul, as Becker sees him, is certainly open to the charge of being anti-Jewish, and the conversion would appear to have separated Paul from his Hebrew religion. As aware as Becker is of Paul's passion for Christ and the crucial importance he placed on the Gentile mission, Becker's work challenges a turn in Pauline scholarship after World War II that has sensitized readers to the Jewishness of Paul. But it was not the Holocaust only, as Marion Soards notes in his introduction to Becker's work,[7] but also an impressive body of Qumran scholarship that has increasingly scrutinized the portrait of Judaism offered by Pauline scholars.

If Becker's reading of Paul is correct, there is every reason to speak of Paul the convert *from* Judaism *to* Christianity. However, the tenacity with which Paul holds on to his Jewish identity in 2 Corinthians 11:22, Romans 11:1, and elsewhere contradicts Becker's placement of Judaism in Paul's rejected, dark past, and calls for an alternative understanding of Paul's "conversion." The real difficulty is that Paul nowhere ever uses the term *Christian,* and there is no indication in the letters that he ever repudiates his native religion.

CALL, NOT CONVERSION

At the opposite end of the spectrum are those who would reject the use of the word *conversion* altogether as it applies to Paul. Certainly, it applied to the Gentile crossover from Hellenistic popular religion to this messianist movement, but it can hardly refer to Paul. In a tour de force, Krister Stendahl has argued that "the usual conversion model of Paul the Jew who gives up his former faith to become a Christian is not the model of Paul but ours."[8] When talking about Paul, he would have us refrain entirely from using conversion language. Stendahl aptly points out that Paul's call to his mission to the Gentiles more closely resembles the call of Isaiah, not the conversion of Augustine. In one of the Servant Songs of Second Isaiah, the prophet speaks of the servant's call: "The LORD called me from the womb, from the body of my mother he named my name" (Isa. 49:1, RSV). Then the servant is given a commission: "I will give you as a light to the Gentiles [as Jews of Paul's era would have understood the Septuagint reference to *ethnē* and the Hebrew *goyim*], that my salvation may reach to the end of the earth" (49:6, my trans.). Jeremiah speaks similarly of his own call: "Before I formed you in the womb I knew you, and before you were born I consecrated you; I appointed you a prophet to the Gentiles" (Jer. 1: 5, my trans. from RSV). This language seems to be echoed in Paul's own autobiographical account in Galatians: "When he who had set me apart before I was born and called me through his grace, was pleased to reveal his Son to me, in order that I might preach him among the Gentiles, I did not confer with any human being" (Gal. 1:15–16, my trans.). Nowhere in this language is there any suggestion that Paul renounced his native faith for a new one, or that he was overcome with a burden of guilt, as in Augustine, that was lifted.

Similarly, Stendahl points out that the three accounts in the Acts of Paul's dramatic change effected by Christ's epiphany on the road to Damascus were in no sense a conversion in the classic sense. Paul did change from persecuting to being an advocate for the church, but he did not renounce the Israelite religion. In fact, chapter 9 follows the pattern we see in the letters where, after the epiphany, Paul is commissioned as an apostle to the Gentiles. Ananias, a pious Jew, is sent to tell Paul he is a chosen instrument: "Go, for he is a chosen instrument of mine to carry my name before the Gentiles" (Acts 9:15 RSV). When these three accounts of the same event are seen to refer to a commission to the Gentile mission and *not* to the remission of a heavy burden of guilt, then it is clear that they are not portrayals of a conversion in the classic sense.

In spite of Stendahl's powerful argument (as also Johannes Munck before him and others, such as Lloyd Gaston, Paul Meyer, and John Gager after him) the application of conversion language to Paul's commissioning has not gone away. Is it possible to make a virtue of this necessity? (By my count, at least forty articles in scholarly journals and monographs have appeared in the past fifteen years on Paul's conversion.) Can this vague word come to have any significance in reference to Paul? At least a couple of possibilities exist.

CONVERSION AS TRANSFORMATION

Beverly Gaventa in *From Darkness to Light: Aspects of Conversion in the New Testament* offers a definition of *conversion* that is much more nuanced than those above.[9] Gaventa allows for a tripartite definition of conversion, one gradual or evolutionary out of previous experience, another a radical repudiation of past "convictions and affiliations," and still another a transformation in which the past is viewed in a totally new way.[10] The third alternative she suggests fits Paul quite well. A Christophany transformed Paul from persecutor to advocate of the church and radically reshaped the way he viewed his native Jewish traditions, scriptures, laws, and customs. This "conversion" was more of a revaluation than a rejection of Paul's Judaism. He now viewed all of the prophets as predictors of Christ, and now in his eschatologically charged present viewed the law in a totally different way. But is such a revaluation a conversion?

I agree with Gaventa that many things may cause one to view the world and the past in a new way—a flash of insight, a new discovery, a holy encounter, or a historical event pregnant with meaning. But is every such revaluation a conversion?

Alan Segal's important book *Paul the Convert: The Apostolate and Apostasy of Saul the Pharisee* (1990) was influenced by Gaventa's study. Segal sees *conversion* as a very broad rubric under which a great deal of change can be subsumed. "The modern study of conversion," he believes, "shows how conversion can be employed as a technical term within specific limits. It also illustrates the contention that every community develops its own definition of conversion."[11] A Jerusalem priest who sought inclusion in the Qumran community and who fulfilled all of the requirements for full participation would be a convert according to Segal. Simple movement from one circle of piety to another (e.g., from Sadducaism to Pharisaism) would be a conversion.

Likewise, presumably, a Hellenistic Christian who sought to become a regular participant in the Jewish Christian church in Jerusalem would also be a convert. But here the definition of conversion has already begun to break down. Moreover, if the definition of conversion is specific to each community, is it still possible to develop a scholarly definition that is more skeptical of indigenous definitions? If one's definition of conversion should become so broad as to be specific to each community, would it then be so broad as to be virtually useless?

While Segal agrees with Gaventa that transformation may be called conversion, he goes far beyond Gaventa in allowing for idiosyncratic definitions, and he differs radically from Gaventa about the nature of Paul's conversion. The subtitle of Segal's monograph, *The Apostolate and* Apostasy *of Saul the Pharisee*, assumes that Paul repudiated his native religion and converted to "Christianity,"[12] though to speak of "Christianity" in Paul's lifetime is an anachronism. Moreover, Segal's thesis would be enhanced with a clearer distinction between what Paul experienced and what Gentile participants in Hellenistic and Roman religions experienced when they became followers of Christ. While Paul's messianism perhaps could be accommodated within an apocalyptic Judaism, there was no way the worship of idols could be accommodated within the church or the synagogue. In other words, Paul's life "in Christ" would hardly require a repudiation of Judaism, but a *requirement* of Gentile life "in Christ" was the repudiation of idols or gods once worshiped.

THE BYNUM MODEL: CONVERSION AS INVERSION?

An alternative to the proposals above is Caroline Walker Bynum's model of conversion as inversion.[13] Acutely sensitive to the multivalence of symbol and to the gendered character of all experience, Bynum argues that in Europe in the High Middle Ages men and women in the Christian tradition, who invoked and interpreted the same symbols, lived in a similar setting, and wrote in the same way, also displayed "consistent male/female differences in using symbols."[14]

The analogies that men drew between the motherhood of Jesus and their own maternity obviously involved a metaphorical gender inversion, and it did more. Since the society was rigidly hierarchical, with males occupying positions of power and influence and women positions of service and nurture, this gender inversion involved the voluntary surrender of a privileged position in society to identify with the less advantaged woman. This hierarchical placement of genders was clearly a male construction. It placed the male in an elevated position aligned with the divine Christ; the woman was assigned the weaker, nurturing role, associated with the human Jesus. Bynum shows how the renunciation of the position of authority, privilege, and wealth to identify with the feminine was a conversion. To become woman was "an obvious image of renunciation and conversion"[15] in which ordinary male status was exchanged for extraordinary female status. Whereas men often understood this identification with women as meekness and world renunciation, women understood the term *woman* to refer basically to being human.[16] But women already in the humble state tended not to identify with Jesus as Mother, or at least not in the same way, but viewed themselves as children of the mother Jesus.[17]

Whereas men's symbols and myths emphasized discontinuity, women's symbols and myths stressed continuity. Whereas men inclined to invert social and biological experience and to emphasize opposition and conversion, women normally spoke less of gender reversal and more about the continuity of self.[18] Women's stories record less "adolescent crisis, [and] more childhood vocation than that of men."[19] "Women's myths and rituals tend to explore a state of being; men's tend to build elaborate and discrete stages between self and other."[20] And even when women used male metaphors to refer to themselves (e.g., as prince), they did so without using the metaphor as a symbol of renunciation.[21] From these observations, Bynum concludes that "women did not in their writings play with male and female oppositions; they did not tell their own stories or the stories of other women as reversals or conversions. They did, however, explore and

play in very complicated ways with what femaleness meant in the theological tradition—that is, with physicality."[22] The implications of that conclusion are
rather far reaching:

> Thus *female* was not to women writers primarily paired with *male* as con-
> trasting image. . . . The woman writer's sense of herself as female was less a
> sense of herself as evil or as not male than a sense of herself as physical. And
> women saw the humanity-physicality that linked them to Christ as in con-
> tinuity with, rather than reversal from their own ordinary experience of
> physical and social vulnerability. . . . Thus women reached God not by
> reversing what they were but by sinking more fully into it.[23]

Although it would be inaccurate to say that Bynum strictly limits the use of
the term *conversion* to describe social or gender inversions, it surely is the case
that she sees an appropriate usage of the term that does not imply a repudiation
of one religion for another. She is also aware that the term may refer to a tendency among males to refer to experiences that mark discontinuity and rejection.
But that discontinuity need not be between competing religions. It may also take
place in the domestic, social, or biological spheres. Indeed, in Europe in the Middle Ages the discontinuity was more likely to be social than to be religious.

BYNUM AND PAUL

In three letters, Paul metaphorically refers to his maternal relationship to his
"converts": 1 Thessalonians 2:7; Galatians 4:19; and 1 Corinthians 3:2. Beverly
Gaventa was the first to take seriously the maternal imagery in Galatians and 1
Thessalonians, and her observations must be the starting place for any investi-
gation.[24] She has not sought, however, to relate her discussion of maternity in
Paul's letters to her earlier discussion of conversion. It seems worthwhile to do
so here.

In Galatians 4:19, Paul addresses the Galatians with an endearing diminutive,
"my little children," then adds, "for whom I am again in the pain of childbirth."
Claiming to have given them birth, he now is in labor once more "until Christ is
formed in you." This generative metaphor, as Steve Kraftchick has labeled it,[25]
resembles that of Bernard of Clairvaux, who not only addressed Jesus as mother
but also sought to replicate Jesus' maternal ethos in his own ministry. His correction of an erring monk uses the metaphor of a woman's birthing and nursing
tasks: "I begot you in religion by word and example. I nourished you with milk.
. . . You too were torn from my breast, cut from my womb."[26] In her discussion
of this passage, Bynum contrasts it with statements in the works of many women
writers of the Late Middle Ages. Women writers, she notes, unlike men, "did not
associate mothering so exclusively with nurturing and affectivity."[27] Being advantaged in the social order, males viewed themselves as stewards of the civil and
ecclesiastical order. To identify with women was to metaphorically vacate that

elevated position. Such a metaphorical inversion Bynum sees as a radical act of humiliation that one may appropriately call conversion.

Other similarities exist. Paul, like the males of the Middle Ages, was socially advantaged by his gender. Authority, correction, and power were similarly vested in males. Therefore, Paul's identification with maternal figures—as with that of the monks of the Middle Ages—may represent a significant social and biological inversion. And that inversion may appropriately be called a conversion.

In Galatians 4:19, we have a complex metaphor. Paul speaks not of giving birth to the Galatians but of giving birth to Christ in them! He speaks of multiple births—"I am *again* in the pain of childbirth." What does it mean to suffer birth pains "again"? Does "again" refer to births Paul has given to believers elsewhere, to repeated efforts to form Christ in the Galatians, or to first giving birth to the Galatians in Christ followed by labor to bring Christ to life in them? In light of Paul's own recollection of their pagan status ("Formerly, when you did not know God . . ." [4:8]) and his mission among them ("You know that it was because of a physical infirmity that I first announced the gospel to you" [4:13]), the third possibility is the most likely. The first birth brings the readers into an eschatological world; the second attempts to bring the Galatians into conformity with that world. This metaphor then calls on the addressees to join Paul in reflecting on the relationship between Paul who is the mother, his children, and their conformity with life in Christ.

While this passage emphasizes Paul's motherhood, the picture in the letter as a whole is more complex. At one level Paul defends and exercises authority, and sometimes he uses the language of violence. He claims authority for his apostleship (2:1–21) and lays a double curse on those who preach any other gospel (1:8–9). Likening the scars left on his body by persecution to Christ's marks (*stigmata*) of crucifixion, he solemnly warns, "Let no one trouble me; for I bear on my body the marks of Jesus" (6:17, RSV). He threatens males who supplement his gospel by cutting off their foreskins, that they will be estranged from Christ (5:4, my trans.). He threatens his Corinthian converts with the rod if they continue in their arrogant ways (1 Cor. 4:21). All of these authoritarian gestures of course are rooted in Paul's convictions about his gospel, and they are also consistent with the definition of maleness in Paul's culture.[28] The comparison of these statements with Paul's metaphorical identification with the pregnant woman giving birth in 4:19 is stark. Here he surrenders his claim to superordinancy to perform a fundamental biological task—to give birth. He voluntarily vacates the elevated power position that his gender, his culture, and his apostolic commission bestowed in order to be the mother of his "little children." Paul's invocation of the maternal imagery is part of a larger pattern of the abdication of or definition of power. Twice over he shares Christ's humiliation by entering metaphorically into the cross (2:19; 5:14). In these metaphorical acts of humiliation, Paul obviously finds a basis for the apostolic authority he claims, an authority that at points is contrasted with that of the Jerusalem pillar apostles. This claim on superordinate status does not contradict the surrender of that claim, but if

Bynum is correct, it represents an inversion that males trace to Jesus himself. To that degree at least, it does appear that Bynum's model is applicable to certain aspects of Paul's self-presentation, and is a form of conversion.

The second passage we shall consider is 1 Thessalonians 2:7. Again, I follow Beverly Gaventa, who makes a compelling case for following Nestle's Greek reading: "We became babes among you, like a nurse tenderly looking after her own children."[29] The NRSV follows the American Bible Society's Greek text: "We were gentle among you, like a nurse tenderly caring for her own children." The manuscript evidence for the Nestle reading, however, is compelling. Such impressive textual witnesses as Papyrus 65, Codex Sinaiticus, Codex Vaticanus, Codex Ephraemi (corrected), Codex Bezae (corrected), the Washington manuscript, Codex Boernerianus, Codex Athous Laurae (corrected), and a number of important Greek minuscule manuscripts support reading *nēpioi* ("babes") instead of *ēpioi* ("gentle").[30] Against some, Gaventa dismisses the argument that it is unlikely Paul would have mixed his metaphors—"we became babes" and "like a nurse." She quite correctly notes that Paul consistently mixes metaphors.[31]

Whether Paul means that the nurse cares for her charges like they were her own children, or that the mother cares for her own children as would a nurse is unclear. The terms *nurse* and *mother* are often linked in classical Greek literature as if they were synonymous.[32] What is clear is that Paul here interprets his apostolic mission as a maternal, nursing task. The nurse, because of her service especially among the upper classes, was revered, loved, and honored. Although often, perhaps most often, the nurse was a slave, she is almost always flatteringly portrayed. She cared for the infants in her charge as if they were her own. She nursed them. When the child was weaned, she fed the child on milk and some solid food, often chewing the food into small chunks before placing it in the baby's mouth. Her own garment was often soaked with food dribbled out in the baby's helplessness. She bathed and dressed the baby, came to it when it cried out at night, walked and soothed it, rocked it in her arms, sang lullabies, told stories, amused the child and often taught the child poems, songs, and even a second language. Stories abound of nurses who remain, serving a family into old age. Families often erected monuments to honor the memory of a departed nurse, and inscriptions pledged to keep her memory alive. Greek literature abounds in stories extolling a nurse's legacy.[33] Paul's nursing metaphor, as jarring as it is when applied to a male, may well reflect the inversion suggested by Bynum's model. But it does more than shock. Becoming female in this metaphorical world was an act of denying both the self and the power constructions of the social world. Just as Paul's choice of celibacy underscores his status as a world renouncer, his renunciation of the superordinancy socially prescribed for males, his exchange of that ordinary condition for an extraordinary one, may aptly be called conversion. Such an inversion, however, hardly implies that Paul rejected his native faith.

There are certainly dangers in seeking to apply Bynum's construction to the first century, and the Europe of the Middle Ages differed markedly from the Eastern Mediterranean of the first century C.E. The pluralism of the first century contrasts sharply with the Christian Europe which Bynum studied. For her study, Bynum had writing samples from women concerned with many of the same issues that concerned men, but in the first century we have almost no writings from women that we can compare with those of Paul. A comparison of Paul's own liminal status with the status of monks and nuns in their orders is not only anachronistic but misleading. And Bynum's use of the term *conversion* may itself be idiosyncratic. Yet her insightful work has relevance for the study of the first century.

While Paul's letters would support this reading through the Bynum lens, a generation later Luke configured Paul quite differently in his Acts of the Apostles. There Luke offered not one but three different and separate accounts of Paul's "conversion," all of which point not to his repudiation of his native religion—for in Acts he remained a Pharisee until the end—but to his integration into the Roman imperial order. He is portrayed as a Roman citizen. Gallio, the Roman procurator in Achaia, before whom Paul is arraigned, dismisses all charges against him and pronounces him innocent. The Roman judge before whom Paul is arraigned in Jerusalem not only affirms his innocence but the judge himself almost converts to Paul's religion. In Acts, therefore, we see that Paul moves from being the quintessential convert to being the archetype of responsible citizenship. The *oikoumenē* (entire inhabited world) of Paul and the *oikoumenē* of the Roman Empire were already beginning to merge. As Melito would later note, it was fortunate indeed that God founded the empire and the church at the same time.[34]

Neither Paul's letters nor the Acts portray a Paul who has repudiated his native Judaism. Paul, as I shall insist, was born a Jew, lived as a Jew, and died as a Jew, but care is needed. His understanding of himself as one pushed to the margin by the "pillars" of the Jerusalem church and rejected by hostile Jewish critics led Harnack to portray Paul as a "former" Jew who delivered the Christian religion from Judaism.[35] If what I say here is correct, Paul's metaphors of himself as mother—even while they disclose a radical inversion of domestic, social, and biological roles—allow for continuity between his messianism and his native Hebrew religion. Although Paul was a marginal Jew, he was in no sense an apostate from Judaism.

Chapter 3

Paul as Organic Intellectual

Reshaping Jewish Apocalyptic Myth from the Margins

The engine that drove Paul's radical vision of the "new creation" was his apocalypticism. Folded into that envisioning was Paul's gospel, his self-understanding, his acceptance and proclamation of the crucified Jesus as God's Messiah, his feverish expectation of the imminent end, his perception of the social and political world, his radical hope for an inclusive elect community embracing Jew and non-Jew, slave and free, male and female, and his fervent belief that the first fruits of the new age were already present. The reverse is equally true—that Paul's apocalyptic gospel sprang from his encounter with Christ. Feeling he was commissioned as an apostle through that encounter, Paul struggled to understand and interpret this apocalyptic myth. The level of intellectual energy necessary to negotiate that myth successfully and to respond to his critics was enormous, and in order to meet that challenge it was necessary that he reshape the apocalyptic myths he had inherited to give them practical issue. That interpretation often placed him in sharp conflict with other interpreters who sought to discredit or even to marginalize him. In essence, we see in Paul's apocalyptic gospel his understanding of the margin as a location of radical possibility. His reshaping of the apocalyptic myth offers an example of how to negotiate the margin actively and imaginatively. This chapter will provide a keener appreciation of that process. The narrative frame of the apocalyptic myth into which Paul inserted himself constructed life at the margin—full of trepidation and fear—as the old world was passing away and as the new creation was breaking in, alive with hope and expectation.

Books, sometimes multivolume books, offer critical descriptions of Paul's theology; detailed studies explore Paul's activity as a theologian. Given Paul's single-minded preoccupation with God's activity in the world, such treatments are natural, inevitable, and sometimes even helpful. None to my knowledge, however, deals with Paul the intellectual—even though Paul may be the foremost intellectual of the New Testament. In this essay, I attend to Paul as an organic intellectual. Cornel West, following Antonio Gramsci, offers a nuanced definition of intellectual activity as an *organic* exercise. An organic intellectual, so construed, is a person bringing a high level of intellectual acuity to bear on the practical or social world, bringing parts of the whole into a meaningful connection.[1] Paul's passionate concern for the community, his use of apocalyptic myth to insert these assemblies (churches) into a narrative with a cosmic reach and worldly significance, and the use of his fertile mind to proclaim and interpret his apocalyptic gospel for ever new boundary settings all would seem to entitle us to call him an organic intellectual. In the letters, we can often see his creative and ingenious mind at work addressing his religiously uprooted converts, shaping their identity as the eschatological elect, creating new forms of religiosity, and establishing an ethos for the "saints" in a new community. His skillful blending of activity and ideology was no disengaged, individualistic exercise, but a passionate, involved, and creative work for the world.

While acute intellectual activity is evident at every level of Paul's discourse, for the sake of clarity and brevity I have chosen to focus on only one dimension, namely, the way he, in light of his experience of Christ, translated apocalyptic paradigms, myths, convictions, and topoi to open the elect of God to pagans. The recognition that apocalyptic thinking was less a product of popular folklore than a result of scribal or learned activity supports my view of Paul as an organic intellectual.[2] Moreover, such a consideration of Paul's adaptation of the apocalyptic idiom as a vehicle of radical openness may offer a way out of the scholarly impasse on whether or not Paul was an apocalypticist.

THE SCHOLARLY DEBATE

In 1960, Ernst Käsemann concluded his epochal essay "The Beginnings of Christian Theology" by expressing the hope that his study had convincingly presented "apocalypticism as the mother of all Christian Theology."[3] Käsemann's proposal created an uproar. His *Doktorvater*, Rudolf Bultmann, replied that "Paul's theology and concept of history came not from apocalypticism but out of anthropology, namely, an understanding of human existence." He argued further that while a detemporalized and existential eschatology was the mother of Christian theology, a crude apocalypticism was not.[4] Philip Vielhauer stated emphatically that Jesus' preaching had "nothing in common with Apocalyptic,"[5] and Hans Conzelmann, a former student of Bultmann's, argued that Paul's theology was based on creedal formulations that were in no sense apocalyptic.[6] Willi Marxsen agreed and categorically stated that Paul "was not an apocalypticist."[7] More recently, E. P. Sanders has disputed Käsemann's thesis, suggesting instead that the "conventions of apocalypticism had . . . little influence on [Paul]."[8] Sanders, joined by Robin Scroggs, argues that Paul inherited a structure with apocalyptic coloration but into that structure he poured something else "truly unique and original."[9] And Abraham J. Malherbe's work on 1 Thessalonians, while recognizing some apocalyptic aspects of Paul's letters, has rightly drawn attention to their parenetic aspects.[10] But Malherbe's treatment of 1 Thessalonians as a parenetic letter in which Paul skillfully uses philosophical traditions to instruct those under their influence gives scant attention to the apocalyptic character of 1 Thessalonians.

While some scholars continued to hold that the apocalyptic myth had a central role in Paul's life, Johan Christiaan Beker gave a passionate defense of apocalyptic as the integrating center of Paul's theology. Beker vigorously argued that the deep structure of Paul's thought was apocalyptic, that "the heart of Paul's gospel" was apocalyptic, and that Paul's outlook was "anchored in the apocalyptic world view," which served as "the fundamental carrier of Paul's thought."[11] With force Beker maintained that "The death and resurrection of Christ in their apocalyptic setting constitute the coherent core of Paul's thought."[12] For Beker, apocalyptic was the core, basis, structure, and conduit of Paul's gospel—a dramatic, sweeping claim indeed. Although Beker's work offered a comprehensive defense of the role of apocalypticism in Paul's thought, it hardly ended the dispute.

To this day, scholarly opinion remains divided on the importance of the apocalyptic myth for Paul. For some it is the *magna mater* of Paul's theology, while for others it is a distant cousin or no relative at all. First Thessalonians, which some see as the most apocalyptic of Paul's Epistles, is to others only a parenetic letter. And as for Paul's appeal in 1 Thessalonians 4:16–17 to the parousia of Christ announced by the archangel and signaled with a blast of the trumpet, as well as the promised ascent of the dead and the living to meet the Lord in the air, these appear to some as the apocalyptic nerve center of Paul's gospel, and to others as a trivial vestige of a Jewish apocalypticism lingering in the shadows of Paul's gospel.

This confusion over the significance of the apocalyptic myth in Paul's thinking is caused in part by the radical alterations Paul made in the apocalyptic myth he inhabited. Such changes may give the impression that Paul repudiated apocalypticism, when he merely reshaped it for his own community. Moreover, his resistance to and qualification of the apocalyptic enthusiasm of the Corinthians may cause some to wonder if he abandoned the apocalyptic myth altogether. While it is common these days to acknowledge apocalyptic elements in Paul's thinking, what is less common is an appreciation of the peculiar Pauline application or translation of the apocalyptic vision—the ways Paul challenged the logical, but in his mind mistaken, appropriation of the apocalyptic vision. That turn, I shall argue, was dictated by the context and sprang from the intellectual genius and complexity of the apostle himself. Here I shall note some of the adjustments Paul made in the apocalyptic myth he inherited and attend to some of the ways he redirected the apocalyptic vision of his addressees. In doing so we may see that Paul sought not to tame, or displace, or demythologize the myth, but to provide constraints within which its vital energy could be experienced within a community threatened by an apocalypticism run amuck.[13] We may also observe how Paul sought to revive an apocalyptic vision that to some seemed to have failed.

Everywhere Paul's letters reveal an author who took for granted a pervasive, powerful apocalyptic myth. While one must acknowledge that there was no canonical model of apocalypticism in the first century, and that those who appropriated apocalyptic symbolism enjoyed enormous freedom in its development and application, Paul's apocalyptic ideology and idiom show a family resemblance to that of Qumran in particular. The conviction that the fateful, cosmic contest between the agents of light and the minions of darkness was nearing a conclusive, convulsive climax appears in both (1 Thess. 4:15–17; Rom. 13:11–12; Phil. 4:5; 1QM). Paul's view that the final catastrophe would radically alter or even dismantle the social and political structures of the day resembles that of Qumran. The conviction that the form of this world was passing away (1 Cor. 7:31) and that the struggle between the "children of light" and the "children of darkness" was part of a powerful drama, cosmic in scope and temporal in inception and resolution, was shared by both (1 Thess. 5:5–11; 1QS 3.18–4.18). The anticipated vindication of the "saints" in the impending judgment, hope for a messianic deliverer, and a scriptural warrant for that hope were shared by Paul and Qumran. And although there were profound differences between the Pauline and the Qumran myths (e.g., in the eschatological timetable, in the priestly orientation or lack of it, and in the roles played by Jesus and the Teacher of Righteousness), nevertheless both shared a myth of crisis. While few scholars believe that Paul had firsthand acquaintance with the Dead Sea community, his debt to and skillful appropriation of apocalyptic symbols reveal a fertile mind at work in treating apocalyptic dualism, apocalyptic disassociation, and apocalyptic simplification.

PAUL AND APOCALYPTIC DUALISM

In *Purity and Danger,* Mary Douglas speaks of the use of taboos or rules to establish community boundaries. The more threatened the community, the greater the need to define its borders. The more fixed the borders, the sharper is the contrast between the insider and outsider; and the sharper the contrast, the greater the tensions created by transactions across those boundaries.[14]

Many apocalyptic writings and the Pauline letters reflect those tendencies. The dualism of apocalypticism knows three sets of boundaries: between the world above and the world below (cosmic), between this age and the age to come (temporal), and between the insider and outsider (social). Whether driven by persecution or by repression and exclusion, or by other causes of distress and trauma, the authors of apocalyptic writings reveal the alienation felt by the community, and that alienation is mirrored in its experience of space and time. Thus, the social differentiation between insiders and outsiders is profoundly reinforced by a mythology cosmic in scope and breathtakingly comprehensive in temporal reach.

That this dualism was replicated in a virulent hatred of the Jerusalem priesthood and the Roman oppressors is well documented at Qumran. These same polarities, however, also appear in the Pseudepigrapha: The fallen angels of *1 Enoch* stand opposite the host of heaven (*1 Enoch* 6–20); heaven and Sheol define the polarities of mythic space, where the "prison house of the [fallen] angels" contrasts with the realm of angels and, hence, the sinners with the righteous (21:10); the final, cataclysmic fire below separates the wicked from the redeemed above in the *Sibylline Oracles* (2.285–310). The fate of the righteous is set in *4 Ezra* by the challenge to Roman tyranny declared by the coming messianic kingdom (7:36; 12:32–34), and the nations and their idols are separated from Israel and its God in *2 Baruch* (5:1, 2; 7:2; 13:12; 48:27; 67:2; 72:5; 85:9).

The sense of having one's fate dictated by a final, climactic, fateful struggle so characteristic of these writings is also evident in Paul's letters. The difference is that Paul, and certainly much of the early church with him, believed that the resolution of that struggle was now beginning. God's righteous act was manifested in the victory over death made evident in the resurrection of Jesus. This triumph marked the beginning of God's move to reclaim a creation that manifestly was also being claimed by dark, sinister powers. The human landscape Paul knew was a dreadful place—tyrannized by principalities and powers (Rom. 8:38), fought over by a hostile "god of this world" (2 Cor. 4:4), subjected to death (1 Cor. 15:26, 54–55), enslaved by sin (Rom. 6:20–23), and threatened by Satan (1 Cor. 7:5), demons (1 Cor. 10:20–22), and the rulers of this age. According to Paul's gospel, this dark, demonic hegemony that for some seemed more real, its claims more insistent than the rule of God, was now being overthrown, and the resolution of that final desperate struggle was at hand.

But how did this cosmic mythology infiltrate the discourse of Paul with the community? We know of obvious cases in 1 Thessalonians where he distinguishes those who worship God from those who worship idols (1:6), where he juxtaposes his apostleship and ministry of encouragement (*paraklēsis*) against the ministry of deceit, uncleanness, guile, flattery, and crowd-pleasing gestures of others (2:3–10), where he positions the believer opposite the immoral, passionate, lustful Gentiles (*ethnē*, 4:3–5), and where he compares the "children of the day" with the children of "the night," the wakefulness of believers with the sleep of the unbelievers (5:5–6).

The same differentiation also appears in 1 Corinthians. First Corinthians 1:9 contrasts those called out of the world "into the fellowship of God's son" with the children of this world; 1:18 opposes those "perishing" to those "being saved"; 2:14–15 contrasts the "unspiritual" and the "spiritual," 5:1 the pagans and the believers, 5:7 the old dough and the new, and 6:1–11 the "washed," the "consecrated," and the "justified" with the immoral, idolaters, the greedy, and the abusive. This differentiation is so pervasive in Paul's letters that it hardly needs further documentation.[15]

Paul's dualism is distinguished not by a separation between the insider and outsider or believer and unbeliever but by a tension between separation and inclusion, or between differentiation and diffusion. Paul's adjustment of the boundaries deviates from the usual pattern of apocalyptic writings of his time or apocalyptic communities such as Qumran. By withdrawal from the evil priests in Jerusalem, by physically retreating to the wilderness, and by imposing a strict daily rule, the "sons of light" separated themselves from the "sons of darkness" (1QS 4.7–14). Their rule forbade the pooling of their property with the "men of falsehood" (1QS 9.8–9); it banned any disputation with "men of the pit" (1QS 9.16); it commanded them not to spend a Sabbath near Gentiles (1QS 11.14–15), and it prohibited the selling of clean birds or beasts to the Gentiles (1QS 12.8–9). And this rigorous separation was invoked under the threat of eternal destruction:

> He [the member of the Community] should swear by the covenant to be segregated from all the men of sin who walk along paths of irreverence. For they are not included in his covenant since they have neither sought nor examined his decrees in order to learn the hidden matters in which they err by their own fault and because they treated revealed matters with disrespect; this is why wrath will rise up for judgment in order to effect revenge by the curses of the covenant, in order to administer fierce punishments for everlasting annihilation without there being any remnant. (1QS 5.10–13)[16]

Of course, however powerful the symbolic and metaphorical rhetoric, the separation from outsiders was not absolute. The presence of Greek manuscripts in the Qumran collection suggests some interchange with the dominant culture. The sectarians continued to remit the temple tax. And readmission after a period of discipline could follow expulsion from the sect. Consequently, absolute separation between the insider and outsider was simply impracticable. Ultimately the question was not if there would be social and cultural intercourse between the "poor" and the "other" but what kind and how much of the foreign to admit and appropriate. Certainly the amount of admission and appropriation that Paul was willing to tolerate differed in degree, if not in kind, from that of the Qumran community.

While the threat of an alien symbolic world appeared no less monstrous to Paul than to the Qumran sectarians, his apostleship and his instructions to the churches more freely embraced the separated. Even when varying circumstances dictated sharply differing emphases, his outreach was consistent. His apostolic mission was directed toward outsiders (i.e., "Gentile sinners," Gal. 2:15). He cautioned enthusiastic celebrants of new life in the spirit in Corinth that they were to seek the honor, respect, and "Amen" of the outsiders (1 Cor. 14:16).

In Romans 12:14–21, Paul urged Roman believers not to retaliate against their adversaries but to bless their persecutors, to eschew revenge, to offer food and drink to the hungry and thirsty, and thereby to conquer evil with good. Thematic and linguistic ties between this passage and 13:8–14 suggest a linkage between nonretaliation and love (13:8). Note, for example, Paul's ironic use of the combat motif in 12:21, where he urges upon his hearers an alternative to convention: "Do not be conquered [*mē niko*] by evil, but conquer [*nika*] evil with good." The combat motif recurs in 13:12–24, where Paul again ironically prescribes an "armor of light" for his addressees (13:12) and thus functionally forges a link between the nonretaliation encouraged in 12:14–21 and the love of 13:8–14. Moreover, already in 13:8 Paul has defined the neighbor for whom love is commanded in Leviticus 19:18 (Rom. 13:9), not as an insider, as in Leviticus, but as "the other" (*ton heteron*; i.e., the outsider). And whoever loves the other, Paul notes, already "has fulfilled the law." So once again we see that Paul was careful to make a connection between the commandment to love and obligation to the outsider. If what I am suggesting is correct, Paul is certainly closer to the Matthean command to love the enemy (Matt. 5:44) than is sometimes acknowledged.[17]

But what informed this nonretaliation? Krister Stendahl has shown how the sectarians' certainty of God's imminent visitation and destruction of the foe formed the basis of their view of nonretaliation. The words of the sectary seem to make Stendahl's case: "I will not return evil to anybody, with good will I pursue man, for with God rests the judgment of every living being and he is the one to repay man for his deeds. . . . And the trial of a man of perdition I will not handle until the Day of Vengeance" (1QS 10.17–20). However, at this point the sectary diverged from Paul: "However, I shall not remove my anger from wicked men, nor shall I be appeased, until he carries out his judgment" (1QS 10.20). This nonretaliation was "grounded in the eschatological intensity of the 'eternal hatred towards the men of perdition.'"[18] God's vengeance thus made their vengeance redundant, and each member of the community felt commanded to "love all the sons of light, each one according to his lot in God's plan, *and to detest* all the sons of darkness, each one in accordance with his blame in God's vindication" (1QS 1.9–11, emphasis added). While Romans 12:19–20—with its emphasis on giving food and drink to enemies and in so doing heaping "burning coals of fire on their heads"—shares the apocalyptic spirit of Qumran, the command to love the outsider in Romans 13:8–9 sets Paul off from the Dead Sea community. Evidently Paul realized the danger of the hate customarily inspired by apocalyptic separation and chose another way.[19]

Paul's urban ministry and his Gentile mission may partly explain his modification of conventional apocalyptic emphases on exclusivity. In a radical tour de force, Paul turned the arguments of the conservative faction in Galatia on their head to make way for "Gentile sinners" (Gal. 2:15). Where they would limit access to the community to the law observant, Paul pushed in another direction by recalling an inclusive baptismal formula that embraced Jew and Greek, bond and free, male and female (Gal. 3:28). Even while Paul recognized separation and exclusion from "the present evil age" (1:4) and the immoral from the community (1 Cor. 5:1–13), his Gentile gospel inevitably introduced a high level of ambiguity into the community that provoked resistance.

Romans itself was written at least in part to answer charges arising from Paul's ministry of inclusiveness directed toward "Greeks and barbarians" (1:14). While Paul was concerned with the problems of getting in and staying in, as Sanders argues, he was also intensely involved in developing a protocol for the crossing of boundaries. In a complex sense, he was not interested just in getting in and staying in, but also in an active, positive engagement with the outsider. As Paul puts it:

> To the Jews I became as a Jew, in order to win Jews. To those under the law I became as one under the law (though I myself am not under the law) so that I might win those under the law. To those outside the law I became as one outside the law (though I am not free from God's law but am under Christ's law) so that I might win those outside the law. To the weak I became weak, so that I might win the weak. I have become all things to all people, that I might by all means save some. (1 Cor. 9:20–22)

This active and positive mission to include the excluded expanded the embrace of the apocalyptic myth Paul inhabited, and this mission was not driven, as John G. Gager has suggested, by a failed apocalypticism but, on the contrary, by a continuing feverish expectation of the end.[20]

In 1 Corinthians 5:1–5, these inclusive and exclusive tendencies interweave with some complexity. The situation Paul addressed there concerned a man who was living with his stepmother in what Paul believed, perhaps incorrectly, was an incestuous relationship.[21] The easy tolerance of the religiously enthusiastic congregation appeared to Paul to sanction such boundless behavior. Infuriated, Paul prescribed the deliverance of the man into the hands of Satan "for the destruction of the flesh"—an action aimed not only at separating the deviant but also at defining the community. "Clean out the old yeast," Paul commanded in 5:7, "so that *you* may be a new batch" (emphasis added).

This tension between boundlessness and boundedness, as Victor Turner has noted, is characteristic of the liminal stage of ritual and myth as well. Following the mythic structure developed by Arnold van Gennep,[22] Turner shows how in the liminal stage tensions are created by competing tendencies: a straining toward universalization (or boundlessness) and a desire to impose structure or limit on the surge toward universalization.[23] Turner's observation aptly describes what we see in 1 Corinthians 5:1–5, where Paul acts to reimpose structure on a community whose spiritual elites sought to rise above all human structures and, therefore, to promote an order that was highly antistructural.[24] As a "ritual of separation,"

Paul pronounced a curse on the offender. The expulsion of the deviant forced the community to engage itself in conversation and to identify itself by ordering its experience through its myths and symbols. This separation of the deviant, however, did not include disengagement from the outsiders (1 Cor. 5:9–10) but from the egregiously offending insider. Here Paul and the charismatic Corinthians were moving in opposite directions. With its cry of liberty, its charismatic fervor, its claim to heavenly wisdom, and its reach for a transsexual, angelic state, the community strained for an apocalyptic resolution that was antistructural, or indeed otherworldly. In asking the community to expel the offender, Paul thus summoned to judgment a people arrogating to itself angelic status. By ritually handing the man over to Satan, Paul asked for community recognition of limits. While Paul's prescription for purging the "old yeast" from the assembly followed the protocol of most apocalyptic writings of the day, he bent the myth to allow for the ultimate rescue of the offender. Even though the severity of his wrong exceeded the wildest pagan debauchery, Paul held out hope that "his spirit may be saved in the day of the Lord Jesus" (1 Cor. 5:5 RSV). The "day of the Lord Jesus" in Paul refers to God's final act of righteousness at the parousia of Jesus (1 Cor. 1:8; Phil. 1:6, 10; 2:16; 1 Thess. 5:2; et al.). Thus, his hope for the salvation of the offender on that day argues against the view that Paul expected the shock of expulsion to precipitate his repentance and rehabilitation.[25] Instead, as in 1 Corinthians 3:14–15, Paul here expressed the hope that in the judgment God would preserve authentic expressions of life in the Spirit in spite of misguided, dirty deeds.

This inclusive gesture contrasts dramatically with Qumran praxis, where final expulsion offered no possibility of reinstatement. Likewise, Revelation eagerly anticipates the total destruction of the enemy without and the deviant within: "Anyone whose name was not found written in the book of life was thrown into the lake of fire" (Rev. 20:11–15).

In the tension Paul here fixes between exclusion and inclusion, and between community wholeness and the salvation of the offender, we see a vigorous intellectual encounter with the complex and conflicted situation of an apocalyptic community in confusion. In so redrawing the boundaries of the community, Paul appears to draw back from the harsh implications of an apocalyptic dualism that he seemed to share at other points. The tensions in this passage between exclusion and inclusion are enormous. Driven by contrary impulses in Paul—his strong communal interests and profound hopefulness in God's grace—tensions were created which remain unresolved, and these tensions so skillfully balanced by this profound intellect are endemic to life at the margins.

PAUL'S QUALIFICATION OF APOCALYPTIC DISASSOCIATION

Although John J. Collins favors the definition of apocalypse forged by the Society of Biblical Literature Genres Project, which eschews any essentialist definition, he, nevertheless, agrees with the essentialists that Jewish and Christian apocalypses share tendencies toward disassociation: "Detachment from this world, in the hope of the glory that is above or is to come, is *a common characteristic* of the Jewish apocalypses." In Revelation, he adds, the "impulse to martyrdom, and to the rejection of this world, is intensified by the example of Jesus, who achieved his victory by his crucifixion. The impact of Christ then is to intensify an element that was already present in the Jewish genre."[26] While Collins's view that detachment is a shared feature of apocalypses needs qualification, detachment is common to apocalyptic writings.[27] Certainly the Qumran writings share that tendency, and some would see the same tendency in Paul's letters as well.

Paul's use of "age, world" (*aion*) and "world" (*kosmos*) as separate realities supports the view that Paul shared the disassociation of his native apocalyptic myth. The heavy, symbolic language of the Galatians prescript that Christ "gave himself for our sins to set us free from the present evil age [*ek tou aionos tou enestotos*]" (Gal. 1:4) shows a drift toward disassociation.[28] Likewise, participation in the cross of Christ crucified believers to (or separated them from) the world (*kosmos*) and the world to (or from) them (Gal. 6:14). Furthermore, salvation was rescue from the chaos and confusion of a world in its final decline: "The present form of this world [*to skēma tou kosmou toutou*] is passing away" (1 Cor. 7:31). Since "the appointed time has grown short," Paul urges "those who deal with the world [to act] as though they had no dealings with it" (7:29, 31a). He likewise urged the Roman church not to be "conformed to this world [*to aioni touto*]" (Rom. 12:2), and he reminded the Philippians of their heavenly citizenship or commonwealth (*politeuma*), antithetical to its earthly counterpart (3:20). Paul's letters are suffused with disassociation language.

In this respect, Paul's apocalyptic myth faithfully represents that of almost all other Jewish and early Christian apocalypticism. Yet it is going too far to suggest that Paul's apocalypticism was either physically or psychologically escapist. There is tension in Paul's view sustained by the "eschatological reservation" (Käsemann) that Paul used to qualify apocalyptic enthusiasm. This qualification sharply contradicted the premature apocalyptic resolution claimed by members of the Thessalonian and Corinthian communities. Paul's dilemma was how to announce the inbreaking of God's final act of righteousness while insisting that the final resolution of the redemption of the world remained outstanding. This straining between the present and the future created explosive tensions calling for a creative response.

We gain some insight into Paul's strategy for sustaining that tension in 1 Thessalonians 4:9–11. Here Paul exhorts the God-taught (*theodidaktoi*) to love one another, "to aspire to live quietly [*hēsuchazein*], to mind your own affairs, and to work with your hands [*ergazesthai tais chersin humon*]." In this passage, Paul was hardly following the Epicurean injunction to withdraw from public life for a type of labor or handwork, divorced from politics in the pursuit of honor and freedom.[29] The traditions of Paul's Diaspora synagogue put Paul closer to Philo's outlook than the highly elitist philosophy of Epicurus.

The key to understanding the passage is the decipherment of the term "God-taught" (*theodidaktoi*), which to my knowledge appears only here in ancient literature. Philo frequently used the term *autodidaktos* to refer to the person who learns without a teacher. Unlike the Greek philosophers, who spoke of the *autodidaktos* as the self-made philosopher, Philo used the term to refer to the person receiving wisdom, virtues, or knowledge directly from God and, therefore, needing no human teacher. Isaac, Adam, Noah, Moses, Melchizedek and others he named as *autodidaktoi*. The *autodidaktoi,* according to Philo, were exempted from physical labor and would in the future "enjoy peace that never ends, released from unabating toils" *(Flight* 173). Moreover, the injunction "to live in quietness" (*hesuchia* and cognates), according to Philo, was no admonition to political quietism but rather an eloquent silence coming from a simple reliance on God *(Moses* 1.66), a confident waiting on God by Abraham to provide an animal for the commanded sacrifice *(Flight* 135–36), or even the eschatological rest hovering over the land in the final days *(Rewards* 157). On that day, Philo promises, those mistreating the land will suffer curses, but the land "when she looks around and sees none of the destroyers of her former pride and high name, sees her market place void of turmoil and war and wrongdoing, and full of 'quietness' [*hēsuchia*] and peace [*eirēnē*], and righteousness [*dikaiosunē*], she will renew her youth and bloom and take her rest calm and serene." In no case does Philo use *hēsuchia* (quiet living) to refer to withdrawal from public life.

While no one would suggest that Paul directly appropriated Philo's language or vision, the type of Jewish expression we see in Philo surely represents the outlook of the Diaspora synagogue elsewhere. The simple facts of Paul's biography—born and reared in a Diaspora Jewish setting, a Greek speaker, steeped in the language of the Septuagint—suggest that Paul was influenced by that social and cultural milieu. Whatever their background, as citizens of the new age waiting for the imminent arrival of the Son of Man, the Thessalonians would have been in an unusually strong position to claim a wisdom direct from God that needed no human teacher (note, e.g., 1 Thess. 5:12), and therefore they could already claim "release" from toil (4:11; 5:14). Certain philosophical traditions as well as Jewish Diaspora traditions could have encouraged that response to Paul's gospel.

Faced with this development, Paul coined the word "God-taught" (*theodidaktoi*) to make explicit what was already implicit in *autodidaktos*. He subordinated the possession of divine wisdom to the love command, and he urged the *theodidaktoi* to work with their hands. In this manner, Paul radically recast the traditional meaning of the term *autodidaktos*, and reestablished the connection between the apocalyptic vision and the sweaty arena of daily life. The associated admonition to "keep calm" (*hēsuchazein*) was hardly an exhortation to political quietism, or a repudiation of unseemly for seemly work, but a form of listening or faithful watching appropriate to the arriving eschatological kingdom. Paul thus locates his readers on the margin with himself—standing on the boundary of this world awaiting the new creation. The waiting, as in Philo, was active, and its sphere was social. So in this manner, Paul moved to qualify the apocalyptic disassociation of some Thessalonians and to link the apocalyptic vision with the tasks of this world.

This qualification of the tendency toward apocalyptic disassociation is hardly confined to 1 Thessalonians. In Romans too, Paul reflects on a version of apocalypticism that encouraged withdrawal from the world and repudiation of a dying order. The commands in Romans 13 to "be subject to the governing authorities" (v. 1) and to pay "taxes to whom taxes are due" (v. 7) make sense only if some believers had understood liberation from this world to mean that one should be diffident toward or contemptuous of civil authority.[30] Paul, however, turned the very myth that had been invoked to encourage withdrawal from the world into a mandate for participation in it. So while encouraging the disassociation characteristic of apocalypticism, he was also urging a positive, fruitful participation in this world. Life at the margin was hardly simple, and no quick resolution was offered by an apocalyptic solution.

PAUL'S COMPLICATION OF THE TREND TOWARD SIMPLIFICATION

The mortal illness of a child, the siege of a city, and an emergency at sea all focus human attention and energy on survival. Similarly, most apocalyptic writings are or pretend to be crisis materials that simplify by directing the attention, behavior, and organization of the community toward an emergency. With its insistence on the final triumph of God's righteousness, the restoration of a new world, and the elimination of all vestiges of diabolical forces, Paul's myth of crisis, though far from simple, followed this pattern. Paul's own sense of mission and his understanding of his apostleship were driven in a single-minded way by the conviction that his was the last generation of the world. And although his apocalyptic gospel simplified social structures, deciphered the mystery of historical terror, and solved the enigmas of Scripture, Paul's letters themselves reflect serious disagreements with his addressees over the nature and extent of the simplifying function of his apocalyptic gospel. I shall address here three aspects of this simplification: gender, suffering, and the interpretation of Scripture.

The Simplification of Gender

Turner has drawn our attention to important social changes that occur in the liminal stage. As Turner has it, these myths are seen as "deep mysteries which put the initiand [the one to be initiated] temporarily into close rapport with the primary or primordial generative powers of the cosmos."[31] Sexlessness, which characterized that primordial stage, characterizes the liminal stage as well.[32] In our equation, where the liminal stage equals the transition from the old to the new age, a restructuring of the social and natural world is taken for granted. Like apocalypticism, a liminal myth deals extensively with death and rebirth, with the destruction of the old order and the emergence of the new. First Corinthians is the best example of Paul's struggle with a community attempting to free itself from this transitional phase.

As Paul's letter tells us, the Corinthians so experienced Paul's myth and so identified with the Lord of glory that they claimed to speak the language of angels (13:1) and were able to claim a transsexual status reserved for heavenly beings. Paul's own celibate state may have unwittingly reinforced the Corinthian inclination to celibacy. Under the slogan "It is well for a man not to touch a woman" (7:1)—and implicitly for a woman not to touch a man—celibacy became the norm of the redeemed (7:4).[33] Married couples abstained from sex. Those married to unbelievers inclined toward divorce to maintain their celibacy (7:12–16). The unmarried remained unmarried even while "aflame with passion" (7:8–9). Moreover, the cult reflected the vision the community had of itself as a gender-neutral society. Their modes of dress and the egalitarian expression of charismatic gifts (prophecy, speaking in tongues, etc., in 11:2–6) blurred the distinction between women and men. What Paul had promised the Galatians—that in Christ there is "neither male nor female" (3:28)—became a reality in Corinth, and ironically Paul did not find it to his liking.[34] Thus, for the Corinthians the great human absolute, *eros,* had given way to another great absolute, transsexual or asexual salvation. And the Corinthian experience of the new age cut through a maze of restrictions and complex rules designed and maintained to keep *eros* within the bounds of a given social order. This new androgynous order simplified all human relationships by equalizing them, and served as a radical alternative to complex, confusing cultural patterns.

Even though at one level Paul was a cohort in the development of this Corinthian spirituality, at another level he vigorously resisted and qualified that spirituality. By insisting on the partiality of the experience of the new age, and the proleptic nature of participation in that arriving end time, Paul complicated the Corinthian "wisdom" enormously. Since the full experience of God's rule will be deferred until the parousia of Jesus, believers must, according to Paul, live in the overlap between the present age and the age to come. Consequently, they must share in the tension generated in the overlap of the warring worlds. Even while insisting on the value of celibacy as a charismatic gift (7:7, 32–34), Paul encouraged each married partner to attend to the sexual needs of the other (7:3–6); he advised those with unbelieving partners to remain married and to "consecrate" the marriage through sexual union (7:12–16);[35] he encouraged single members "aflame with passion" to marry (7:8–9); and he admonished them all to acknowledge the distinction between and interdependence of man and woman (11:2–16). By affirming their sexuality they would, in Paul's view, be acknowledging their continued tie to this world. In so qualifying the Corinthians' slogan "It is well for a man not to touch a woman" (7:1), Paul emphasized the transitional character of this dawning new age, deferring full participation in it until the imminent parousia of Christ.[36] The tie thus secured to the world gave the Corinthian myth a measure of realism that the community was dangerously close to forfeiting.

The Interpretation of Suffering

Beyond the simplification of gender and social relationships, Paul's apocalyptic myth offered a simplified understanding of historical terror. Of course, this understanding was hardly new. Since the Maccabean revolt, apocalyptic writings had presented suffering, persecution, and martyrdom as marks of God's people (*Jub.* 23.13–22; *2 Bar.* 70:2–10; *4 Ezra* 5:1–12). First Thessalonians and 1 Corinthians offer immediate confirmation of Paul's place in that tradition even while revealing a simultaneous shift of emphasis away from it.

The cross of Jesus became for Paul an important metaphor through which all suffering and terror received its significance. Paul's own abuse, rejection, and hardship shared mythically in that cross and simultaneously served as a model for the churches. Through that model, the churches participated in the cross and shared in the community of the suffering redeemed. If authentically Pauline, 1 Thessalonians 2:14–16 shows how rejection by their own people ("compatriots") brought the suffering churches in Thessalonica and Judea together into a shared community of suffering.[37] More importantly, in 1:7–10 Paul linked the physical and psychological terror of the Thessalonians with that of believers in Achaia, Macedonia, and beyond. Not only did believers find consolation and hope in this community of suffering; they also found independent confirmation of their membership in the community of the redeemed. As Paul put it, "You yourselves know that this is what we are destined for" (3:3).

Clearly the Thessalonians found other interpretations of their suffering too immediate and too insistent to be ignored. The death of baptized friends raised questions about the truth of Paul's gospel, since it had led some to expect that all believers would live to welcome the returning Lord. Their own persecution inevitably raised questions about the delay of the return, and about signs of the return (4:13–5:11). With hope flickering, the temptation was great to return to old, familiar ways (4:5–8). Fearing for their steadfastness, Paul dispatched Timothy to remind them of his teaching given "beforehand" (3:2–4) and to reassure them "so that no one would be shaken by these persecutions" (3:3). By recalling his own suffering and insults in Philippi (2:1) and strong opposition in Thessalonica (2:2), Paul emphasized the bond between himself and his readers. And by recognizing that their reception of the word brought "much oppression" (1:6, my trans.) and that this suffering was also shared by churches in Judea (2:14), their community of suffering was extended to embrace the mother church itself. In their misery they gained company. And by refracting this experience through the death of Christ, Paul gave the chaos and confusion, dislocation, and death experienced by the Thessalonians (4:13–18) a transcendent holiness (see also 2 Cor. 4:7–12). Cosmic arrhythmia and decay became a prolepsis of the new age. Cataclysm was suffused with divine presence because the woes, like birth pangs, heightened the expectancy of the arrival of the new age. The more intense the trauma, the more chaotic the confusion, the brighter the hope!

Similarly, in 2 Corinthians Paul speaks of the simplifying function of suffering. Even the acrid stench of the martyr's corpse found its micromimesis in the daily afflictions of life "in Christ." Their suffering, like that of Christ, became a prolepsis of the salvation of the world and proof of their own salvation. As Paul says, "We are the aroma of Christ to God among those who are being saved and among those who are perishing; to the one a fragrance from death to death, to the other a fragrance from life to life" (2 Cor. 2:15). Through this pact with death, established in the mythical experience of the death of Christ, Paul sought to link the alienation and distress of the community with the source of all meaning and life. Thus, Paul's myth ordered a chaotic world, and in doing so reinforced the community. And through its own suffering—either at the hands of such cosmic powers as death or from such human agents as one's own tribal associates—community solidarity was secured. In this sense, the social alienation and cosmic distress imbued the margin with an apocalyptic urgency, and the apocalyptic lens offered a way of seeing the world, a mode of being that was alive with possibility.

Earlier in 1 Corinthians, Paul dealt with a situation brought about more by internal forces than by external competitors. Perhaps through a misunderstanding of Paul, the Corinthians claimed a total experience of salvation that was profoundly escapist. Paul's insistence on the incompleteness of the salvific process and the link he forged between the Lord of glory and the cross challenged the Corinthian identification. Paul's call to participate in the brokenness of this world with its human pain and incompleteness (1 Cor. 1:12–13) questioned the Corinthian escapism.

The complexity and tension that Paul interjected into the Corinthian myth can easily be seen in chapter 4. In verses 9–16 Paul offered a brutally sarcastic contrast of the hurt and abuse he and his coworkers endured with the religious puffery of the Corinthians. The apostles, he noted, were exhibited by God as "last of all" (4:9), like persons under a death sentence, as spectacles to the world and angels, as fools, weak, dishonored, vulnerable, hungry, naked, thirsty, knocked about, toiling, cursed, slandered, treated like garbage and everyone's offscouring. His own experience contrasted dramatically with the claims of the "pneumatic" Corinthians to be wise, free, sated, powerful, rich, mature, invincible, glorified, resurrected participants in the superior order of heavenly beings.

By citing his own humiliation and calling on his "children" to imitate himself (4:15–16), Paul used his authority as father and as suffering apostle to qualify the claims of the Corinthians, and he did so without explicitly denying their pneumatic existence. As Paul stated elsewhere, the primeval symbiosis between *Endzeit* and *Urzeit* was anticipated in Christ, but the full realization of that embrace remains outstanding (Rom. 8:22–23). One's hope in that imminent resolution established one's place in the eschatological drama, but the deferral of that resolution left one firmly involved in the swirl of confusion and dislocation endemic to human suffering and incompleteness. Thus, we see the same tension between apocalyptic simplicity and complexity that informed Paul's insistence on a simultaneous disassociation from and involvement in the world.

The Interpretation of Scripture

While the least ambiguous trend toward simplification may be seen in Paul's apocalyptic interpretation of Scripture, here also tension is evident. All scriptures, according to Paul, found their fulfillment in the arriving rule of God manifested in the death, resurrection, and return of Jesus. And while the methods of interpretation were ingenious and complex, and sometimes circuitous and convoluted, their destination was rarely in question. Abraham's seed is Christ (Gal. 3:16), Paul claimed. The archetypal Adam of Genesis has an antitype in Christ (Rom. 5:12–21). David's line gains its culmination in Jesus (Rom. 1:4). Sarah and Hagar find their counterparts in the children of the Spirit and the children of slavery (Gal. 4:22–28). The prophets, likewise, already anticipated the new age inaugurated in Jesus' death and resurrection. Of Paul's approximately forty references to or quotations from the prophets, all in one way or another apply to the dawning *eschaton*.[38] The prophets, Paul believed, predicted the apocalyptic era now dawning (e.g., Rom. 1:2; 16:26). They foresaw the turning to the Gentiles in the last days (Rom. 3:29; 9:25–26; 10:20; 15:12). Their murder foreshadowed the death of Jesus (1 Thess. 2:15), and their pronouncements forecast his elevation and return.

As with the Prophets, so with Torah and the Writings, Scripture was unfailingly experienced as a treasure of wisdom and knowledge of the future which only now was yielding up its secrets. So while the mechanics of Scripture interpretation were complex, the outcome of the exegesis was predetermined. Light from the apocalyptic myth illumined the secret wisdom of the Scriptures and then was refracted back onto the community sharing the myth. From the end of the world back to the text and then back to the world again the loop ran. In this orbit, through the text the myth of crisis gained a richer texture, a deeper substance, and a sacred framework. In this circle, the community shared in the life of the text, and the text shared in the fabric of the community. The hermeneutical circle was initiated, then, through the myth of crisis. Through the vantage point given by the apocalyptic myth, the community gained a perspective on the whole of Scripture and its place in it. Thus, the myth cracked the code, finding the key to the text's secrets. In turn, the text validated the myth. "Indeed," Paul says, "to this very day whenever Moses is read, a veil lies over their minds; but when one turns to the Lord, the veil is removed" (2 Cor. 3:15).

This is hardly to say that tension was absent from Paul's interpretation of Scripture. Perhaps nowhere is this tension more apparent than in Romans 9–11, which, as I noted above, still practically pulses in a reader's hands. The tension was created by the dialectic of an apocalyptic myth based on the promises of God to Israel that in fact embraced "Gentile sinners" (Gal. 2:15). The question raised by the inclusion of the Gentiles who had accepted the gospel was whether God had excluded the Jews who had rejected the gospel. If so, what would that imply about this God? Had he reneged on his promises to Israel? Had his word failed (Rom. 9:6)? Perhaps nowhere in Paul's letters is such a profusion of scriptural passages summoned to address a single issue. This dazzling array of Scripture reinforces one's sense of the gravity and difficulty of Paul's argument.

The argument pulls in contrary directions—affirming first God's freedom to include Gentiles qua Gentiles, even if that means rejection for Israel, and second, somewhat paradoxically, God's firm commitment to Israel's salvation. Citing Genesis 18:10, 14, and 25:23, Paul justifies the inclusion of Gentiles by showing how God has always chosen to bless some and not others, preferring Isaac over Ishmael, Jacob over Esau, and even Joseph over his brothers. Citing Exodus 33:39; 9:16; and Isaiah 29:16, and alluding to a number of other passages, Paul responds to the question: If God acts so arbitrarily, rejecting the chosen and choosing the rejected (9:14), hardening the heart of some and making others receptive (9:19), how can Israel be faulted for rejecting the gospel? In 9:25–29, Paul strings together citations from Hosea 2:25; 2:1; Isaiah 10:22; Hosea 2:1; 11:5; Isaiah 28:22; Deuteronomy 5:28; and Isaiah 1:9 to respond to the question about the justice of God. Is God just, Paul allows his objector to ask, if God includes Gentiles who did not pursue righteousness and excludes Israel who did pursue righteousness? Citing Isaiah 28:16, Paul notes that in its contest for righteousness Israel stumbled over a stone placed on the track by God (Rom. 9:33)![39] Just when it appears that Paul's sports metaphor disqualifies Israel from the race, however, he returns with a rhetorical question: "I say, therefore, has she stumbled so as to fall?" and answers emphatically, "Absolutely not!"

Near the end of his discussion Paul concludes: "So that you may not claim to be wiser than you are, brothers and sisters, I want you to understand this mystery: a hardening has come upon part of Israel, until the full number of the Gentiles has come in. And so *all Israel will be saved*" (Rom. 11:25–26). At this point, Paul tilts against the expectation in sports that winners require losers. Since the Gentiles have won, one expects the Israelites to lose. But Paul's answer is surprising. Both the Gentiles who did not race and Israel who stumbled but recovered are winners.

The tension between these two contradictory assertions reaches the breaking point when Paul acknowledges that the question of how this can be accomplished finds no human resolution. The answer according to Paul is hidden in the mystery of God's own being. Paul can only wonder at it as he launches into a concluding, soaring benediction (11:33–36):

> O the depth of the riches and wisdom and knowledge of God! How unsearchable are his judgments and how inscrutable his ways!
>
> > "For who has known the mind of the Lord?
> > Or who has been his counselor?"
> > "Or who has given a gift to him,
> > to receive a gift in return?"
>
> For from him and through him and to him are all things. To him be the glory forever. Amen.

Once again the tension in Paul's own gospel extended his logic to the breaking point. God will include Gentiles, while remaining faithful to his promises to

Israel. The tension between these bold affirmations finds a resolution only in the future, and even then only in the divine mystery. So while Paul's scriptural interpretation found a simplification when refracted through the lens of his apocalyptic myth, his hermeneutic was complicated by inclusive tendencies set loose by his gospel.

CONCLUSION

In this discussion of the tension in Paul's apocalyptic eschatology and of his mastery of the idiom, I have observed the organic nature of Paul's intellectual activity. I have noted creative applications of the idiom in its transfer from both Jewish and messianic sources. I have pointed to the tension in Paul's thought both with the idiom that he used and within the fresh constructions he created. His attempt to correct the eschatological enthusiasm at Corinth, his efforts to encourage, to reassure, and to exhort those in danger of disillusionment at Thessalonica, and his insistence on the inclusiveness of his apocalyptic gospel in Rome all involved him in applications fraught with tension and ambiguity.

But how was the tension in Paul's apocalypticism different from that endemic to all apocalypticism, since all apocalypticism creates tension between two worlds? There always exists a tension in apocalypticism between this world as known through suffering and incompleteness and another world as known only through apocalyptic metaphor and myth. And the greater the enchantment with the other world, the greater the disenchantment with this world. In a world in which oppressive inertia holds sway, apocalypticism envisions change—radical, dramatic, revolutionary, convulsive change. A heightened awareness of a common danger and the deficiencies of all human systems inspire the seer's vision of a brighter world. The greater the sense of deprivation and loss, the more painful is the conflict between the chaos of this world and the regeneration of the next, between helplessness and vindication, between the odor of death and the aroma of the new creation. That vision challenges accommodations to cultural norms, to political ideology, to institutional intransigence, and to the idols of the day. That vision judges complacency at the plight of the vulnerable, the distress of the victims, and the agony of the brutalized. And that vision offers consolation and hope to the marginalized visionaries. Inevitably such a vision creates tension. So how is the tension in Paul's version of apocalypticism different?

While all of these tensions exist in Paul's apocalypticism, they are compounded and heightened by added tensions. First, there are tensions between himself and congregations who seek escape from this world through absorption into the world to come. (All apocalypticism, including that of Paul, encourages disassociation, but Paul, while allowing for disassociation, will not tolerate disengagement from the world.) Then there are tensions between him and the exclusivist tendencies inherent in apocalyptic myth. (All apocalypticism, including that of Paul, draws sharp boundaries between the insider and outsider, but Paul's emphasis on love for the outsider requires a protocol for crossing those boundaries to embrace the persecutor. This emphasis introduces a high level of ambiguity into the boundary question: Absolutely secure boundaries mitigate against change; adjustable or open boundaries make change possible but foster ambiguity; obviously decisions about the location and symbolic significance of boundaries make a difference in the way a tradition will grow.) Finally, there are tensions between God's gospel to the Gentiles and the historic promises to Israel. (All apocalypticism divides the custodians of the mysteries from the ignorant or incredulous, and so does Paul, except that Paul refuses to agree that the inclusion of Gentile sinners implies the exclusion of Israel. The tension of this paradoxical vision finds its resolution only in the future and in the mystery of God.)

Inevitably, to highlight the importance of the continuing tension in Paul's appropriation of the myth he inhabits is to caution against making the implied resolution—the future—the modus operandi for understanding Paul's present. As critics, we do well to use restraint in supplying for Paul's myth a resolution that he himself can only anticipate.[40] Stories as we tell them may require a resolution, as do symphonies. But the full resolution of God's story (*mythos*) Paul never knew. The resolution of God's story he only dimly apprehended, even though he fully inhabited it. And that tension was experienced and prescribed by Paul as a continuing condition. It was this complexity, outreach, and tie to this world that made it possible for transition, or liminality, to become a permanent condition. This combination avoided the eschatological disappointment of the enthusiasts and the easy conformity and surrender to the status quo of the traditionalists. So in the vitality of Paul's thought, in the skillful adaptation of his native apocalyptic idiom, and in his creative interpretation of his apocalyptic gospel for a variety of contexts, we see an organic intellectual at work on the margin.[41]

Chapter 4

Death and Resurrection

A Theology Forged at the Margins (2 Corinthians)

In this chapter I explore ways theological language was used to marginalize and to discredit Paul and his gospel, and the way he owned that marginal status as a location for radical revision. I follow Georgi's thesis that the attacks on Paul came from rival Hellenistic Jewish apostles. I also note how Paul appropriates the language of human frailty and mortality—and of Jesus' death and resurrection—to meet the challenge of his rivals. I explore Paul's ironic use of metaphor to expose the attempts of his competitors to gloss over the tragic dimension of human experience and divine intervention. I also show how Paul's theology of resurrection was fabricated on the anvil of crisis in response to attempts from his competitors to create a theology of glory that, had they won, would have dramatically altered the nature of the Gentile mission. While it is tempting to characterize his rival Hellenistic Jewish "super-apostles" as challengers on the left and his critics from Jerusalem as adversaries on the right, I see a flaw in that description. It falsely locates Paul at the center. Our post facto constructions do often place Paul at the center, but that is anachronistic. In his own day, Paul's rivals pushed him to the margin by portraying him as a dangerous innovator whose gospel was an outrageous novelty. This chapter shows how Paul accepted that marginal status as an instrument of radical possibility.

BACKGROUND OF PAUL'S RESURRECTION THEOLOGY

Just as language magically and particularly revealed and shaped the identity of Helen Keller, so the language of Paul's tradition also influenced his persona and experience. Far from being a passive mirror of his outer world or spontaneous expression of his inner world, language itself shaped Paul's world. Language formed and informed his understanding of God, Christ, time, church, and his own mission.[1] Similarly, Paul's experience of and thinking about the resurrection owed much to the language of his native Judaism and early Christianity. It was not Paul's experience of Christ but his Pharisaism (Phil. 3:6) and his Jewish apocalypticism that first bequeathed to him a resurrection language. From the Maccabean revolt to the first century, persecution, martyrdom, and a belief in the resurrection were correlates in Jewish apocalypticism. Just as Daniel declared, "Many of those who sleep in the dust of the earth shall awake, some to everlasting life, and some to shame and everlasting contempt" (12:2), so also after the revolt the author of 1 Maccabees announced God's vindication of the martyrs through the resurrection (5:37; 7:19; 13:7). Furthermore, in Jewish apocalyptic literature generally, judgment, resurrection, and God's vindication of the righteous all collaborated to offer a discourse of escape, comfort, hope, and consolation to the oppressed. That outlook clearly informed Paul's citation of Hosea 13:14 (LXX) in 1 Corinthians 15:55 to express his confident, triumphant hope that God raises the dead.

After and perhaps even before Paul's apostolic call, the early church joined Judaism as his tutor in the language of faith. Rudolf Bultmann held that the Hellenistic church was the "historical presupposition of Paul's theology,"[2] and Paul's conviction that God raised Jesus from the dead had its genesis in those early resurrection traditions (Rom. 10:9; 1 Cor. 6:14; 15:15; 1 Thess. 1:10). Likewise, Paul's recognition of the salvific character of the resurrection ("he died *for* all . . . and was raised for them," 2 Cor. 5:15) predated his apostolic call. Although the Hellenistic church had no unified theology, Paul was, as Bultmann held, doubtless influenced by aspects of its thinking. In addition, however, Paul's citation of resurrection traditions also recalls the kerygma of early Christian apocalypticism. It is important to realize, therefore, that Paul's theology of the resurrection has deep roots in his Jewish tradition.

CONTEXT OF PAUL'S RESURRECTION THEOLOGY

As important as these traditional elements were in Paul's theology, it was in response to crises in the churches that Paul's own theology of the resurrection developed. These heated exchanges forced Paul to think through, to refine, and to interpret his views. It is mistaken, therefore, to paste together elements from all of the letters to form a resurrection collage, for Paul offers us no comprehensive, systematic view of the resurrection. While some elements appear consistently in

Paul's view of the resurrection, we best learn what he thinks about the resurrection by noting how he engages specific situations. In 1 Thessalonians, for example, we find one such concrete application. After enthusiastically embracing Paul's gospel, many Thessalonians believed they would survive to welcome Jesus' parousia, but the unexpected death of believers left them stunned and confused. Puzzlement about the fate of the deceased led some to doubt Paul's gospel. Some grieved as if they had no hope (1 Thess. 4:13), and others were tempted by former pagan behavior (1 Thess. 4:3, 7). Paul responded to this erosion of faith by emphasizing Jesus' parousia as a necessary consequence of his resurrection (1:10; 4:10, 14). This emphasis on Jesus' resurrection and his promise of a reunion with departed loved ones at Jesus' parousia (1 Thess. 4:17–18) aimed to offer consolation and hope to the grief stricken.

In 1 Corinthians, Paul unfolded his teaching about the resurrection in dialogue with religious enthusiasts claiming angelic status *hic et nunc*. These enthusiasts either claimed they were already raised and therefore in need of no future resurrection, or they shared a Greek aversion to the body that made the idea of the resurrection of the body repulsive. In any case, Paul responded to their denial of the resurrection (1 Cor. 15:12) by linking the fact of the resurrection of believers to the tradition of Jesus' death and resurrection (1 Cor. 15:4). In writing to the church at Rome, Paul, after being stung by charges that his law-free gospel encouraged libertinism, separated dying with Christ (in baptism) from rising with Christ (in the future) to emphasize the continuing ethical struggle that is necessary to bear witness to life's newness (Rom. 6:1–5).

Because of the linkage Paul forged between Jesus' death and resurrection in 2 Corinthians, and the way he used that linkage to challenge a theology of glory and success, I shall spend most of the remainder of the chapter discussing it. This teaching arose in competition with rival missionaries whom Paul, with biting sarcasm, calls "super-apostles" (2 Cor. 11:5; 12:11), "false apostles" (11:13), and minions of Satan (11:13–15). The sharpness of Paul's attack reveals the success these opponents enjoyed with the Corinthians. Their powerful gospel, inspired Scripture interpretation, miraculous deeds, and radiant Christlike personalities caused Paul and his gospel to suffer by comparison. Although the identity of these menacing adversaries is much disputed, the general features of their profile are recognizable.[3] They claimed to be apostles of Christ with powerful spiritual gifts (10:5; 12:11). They proudly appealed to their status as Hebrews, Israelites, and descendants of Abraham. These "servants of Christ" (11:22–23) carried letters testifying to the wonderful success their gospel enjoyed elsewhere (3:1). They appealed to divine epiphanies (12:1–5), they proudly displayed their vaunted, superior wisdom (1:12), and for their ministry they accepted money. Apparently they also expected the physique and bearing of an apostle of Christ to reflect the glorious presence of the divine redeemer. Their emphasis on the Christian life as a dynamic, immediate eschatological reality minimized the importance of the cross.

The sharp contrasts Paul drew between himself and his opposition supports this sketch so finely drawn by Dieter Georgi.[4] To distinguish his gospel and apos-

tleship from that of his rivals, Paul commonly introduced contrasts with nega-
tions (e.g., *ou* or *mē* ["not"]) followed by a strong adversative *alla* ("but"). Note,
for example, 1:9, 12, 24; 2:17; 3:1, 3, 12; 4:5, 18; 5:15; 10:13, 18.[5] In
2 Corinthians, Paul confronts his critics as "hucksters" (2:17), who with "letters
of recommendation" (3:1) were lording it over the Corinthian church (1:24),
boasting in appearances (5:12), claiming superior wisdom (1:12) and sufficiency
(3:5), and fixing on evidence of the power of their gospel (4:18). He accuses them
of preaching themselves (4:5) and of living for themselves (5:15). Although all of
Paul's contrasts do not simply envisage him and his antagonists (especially those
in 2:4–5), most do; as such, they reveal the flashpoints between him and the rival
apostles. The climate created by these opponents prompts in 2 Corinthians one
of Paul's most powerful theological statements about the resurrection, and one
which is apposite to the church today, especially in North America.

Paul wrote 2 Corinthians to a congregation that once had enthusiastically welcomed him but had since shifted its affections, love offerings, and devotion to
traveling missionaries instead. Increasingly, the Corinthians had come to suspect
Paul's motives (11:7–11), to question his gospel, and to compare him unfavor-
ably with the visiting apostles (12:11). They belittled his apostolic gifts and
accused him of duplicity and cowardice: duplicity because while refusing direct
contributions, he promoted an offering for Jerusalem, which they suspected he
was using to line his pockets (12:16–17); and cowardice because earlier, when he
had made a hasty visit to correct their mistaken impressions, a painful shouting
match (2:1) had led to his hasty retreat. Then, from a safe distance Paul had written a bitingly sarcastic "tearful letter" (2:4). Some mocked Paul's "brave" defense.
They said, "His letters are weighty and strong, but his bodily presence is weak,
and his speech contemptible" (10:10). These attacks were apparently deliberately
designed to marginalize Paul and to subvert his gospel, and they obviously gained
some credence with the Corinthian church. Suspicious and contemptuous of
Paul, the Corinthians seemed all too willing to follow the more glamorous gospel
of the new apostles and to prefer their spirituality and radiant personalities to
Paul. Within this context, full of acrimony and suspicion, Paul crafted a theology of the resurrection, a theology suffused with irony and ambiguity.

RESURRECTION IN THE THANKSGIVING (1:3–11)

To those apostles who ridiculed Paul for his physical infirmity, derided him for
being "untrained in speech" (11:6), and suggested that he and his gospel exuded
unpleasant odors (2:14–17), Paul embraced their characterization and turned it
to his advantage. Granting that he was weak and unimposing, that his body was
decaying, and that he was unskilled in speech or rhetoric, Paul read his experience in light of the cross and simultaneously questioned the sense of immediacy
created by his rivals' absorption in a new age spirituality that emphasized the resurrected life at the expense of the cross. In response to his critics, Paul

concentrated on what are valid proofs of the resurrection, and how to read human experience if it is one of those proofs. Paul knew that human experience, rather than coming naked or uninterpreted, must be deciphered in light of something else. For Paul's rivals, that something else was evidently the glorified Jesus; for Paul, that something else was ironically the suffering and dying Jesus.

In a much broader and deeper sense than oriental Hellenism ever imagined, Paul embraced the margin and found in it a radical possibility. He insisted that the experience of life came through death.[6] Life is seen *in* death, Paul insisted, not *after* death as an automatic and natural sequitur, and not in the denial of death as a real power in the present. Paul's own experience, he claimed, was evidence of that truth. His physical weakness, ineptitude, bruises, and scars received their explanation or even sacralization through the physical suffering of the dying Savior. Ambiguous in their bare form, therefore, afflictions could be read either as signs of weakness, alienation, mortality, baseness, failure, and even divine rejection; or they could be viewed as symbolic participation in the death of Jesus (4:10). In the Corinthian letters more than anywhere else, Paul interprets human weakness, affliction, and decay as an epiphany of the resurrected Lord.[7] From the very beginning of 2 Corinthians, Paul telegraphs his intention to view the dark side of human experience.

Although the opening thanksgiving appears in all of Paul's letters except Galatians, the blessing in 2 Corinthians constitutes a variation on the usual Pauline thanksgiving. James M. Robinson has discussed this variation, noting how Paul creates a hybrid form by grafting elements from a liturgical tradition onto the traditional thanksgiving (see especially 1:3: "Blessed be the God and Father of our Lord Jesus Christ").[8] There Paul recalls how his suffering participates in the suffering of Christ and leads to divine consolation (1:5). He assures the Corinthians that their suffering too would bring God's consolation (1:6). Autobiographical information about his brush with death in Asia Minor and about suffering so oppressive that it left him despairing of life itself provide the very human location of his first appeal to the resurrection tradition in 2 Corinthians: "Indeed, we felt that we had received the sentence of death so that we would rely not on ourselves [in contrast to his rivals] but on God who raises the dead" (1:9).[9] While this reference to the resurrection is entirely traditional, its parsing of death and pointed application to the Corinthian setting has a distinctive Pauline ring. Here Paul associates this traditional affirmation of God who raises the dead with his own physical weakness and human frailty to counter the hubris of his self-confident rivals who, filled with pneumatic powers, boasted of the superiority and revivifying power of their gospel.[10]

Their experience of the Lord gave the "super-apostles" a sense of invulnerability and sufficiency. Seven times in this letter, Paul either makes pejorative references to those commending themselves (10:12, 18; 3:1) or contrasts his own commendation with that of his rivals (4:2; 5:12; 6:4). (Only four references to self-commendation appear in all of Paul's other letters.) Associated with such self-confidence was a self-sufficiency (*hikanos*) on the part of these false apostles that also disturbed Paul. In 3:5 (RSV), Paul acknowledges his own insufficiency ("*Not that we are sufficient* [*hikanoi*] of ourselves to claim anything as coming from us") and gives credit to God ("our competence [*hikanotēs*] is from God"). And more than in his other letters, Paul emphasizes the foolishness of boasting. (Of the 55 references to boasting in the undisputed Pauline letters, 29 occur in 2 Corinthians.) The proper antidote to such boasting, Paul suggests, is the brutality of the human experience itself. Harsh experiences teach about mortality, and from them Paul learned to depend on God who raises the dead. Thus, already in the opening of the letter, Paul signals his intent to use his proclamation of the death of Jesus as the canon by which human experience is judged and the powerful, alluring Hellenistic culture is criticized.[11]

DECIPHERING AMBIGUOUS METAPHORS (2:14–17)

While no explicit reference to the resurrection appears in 2:14–17, it is nevertheless implicit in two metaphors. The first is the metaphor of a Roman triumphal procession, in which triumphant military commanders like Titus led their captives through the streets in shameful display and humiliation.[12] Octavian's profound disappointment in not being able to capture Cleopatra alive to parade her in chains through Rome on his triumphant return is now legendary. Reflecting on his opponents' charge that he is inferior and weak, Paul compares himself and his coworkers to pitiful captives shown off by a victorious army. With this image Paul couples a second metaphor about sweet fragrance and bad odors. From these powerless creatures put on display, so Paul notes, a fragrance spreads out from those "knowing him" (2:14), for, as Paul continues, "We are the aroma of Christ to God among those who are being saved and among those who are perishing; to the one a fragrance from death to death, to the other a fragrance from life to life" (2:15–16). Paul here works as a "strong poet" to effect a change in the Corinthian understanding of a God-forsaken appearance.[13] Although the metaphors drawn from the Roman triumphal procession and from sweet odors and acrid stench enjoy no historical association, they suggest a rhetorical one. If Victor Furnish is correct that 2:14–17 helps introduce a larger discussion of the nature of true apostleship that runs from 2:14 to 5:21, then the mixed metaphors do indeed contain logic of their own.[14] Only a short time before, Paul had struggled with a religious enthusiasm that had threatened to fracture the community in Corinth from the inside. He knew how prone this church was to boast of exclusive truth and pretentious wisdom. From their devotion to Apollos and their request for his return (1 Cor. 16:12), Paul may have suspected that these Corinthians would welcome wandering charismatic apostles with a flashy gospel and perhaps displace him entirely. The wandering charismatics' scorn of Paul's gospel and public attacks on his apostleship provoked this response.

Paul's defense in 2:14–17 answers his rivals from the outside and responds to doubting, suspicious critics from within. The first metaphor asks his readers to examine their sympathies. Would they identify with the triumphant ruler or the defenseless prisoners in the metaphor? Who among the believers in the risen Lord would not recognize the slicing irony of this image? The subjects of the cosmic Lord of history were humiliated by a pagan ruler. Who of his addressees would not eagerly anticipate the coming reversal of the positions of the underdog and the overlord? Thus, this metaphor highlights the ambiguity of power and weakness in this world and in so doing deconstructs the triumphalistic glorification of success of the "super-apostles."

The second metaphor extends the appeal and challenge of the first one. Paul's weakness is like carrion compared to the robustness of the "super-apostles." Paul, however, turns the metaphor against his critics by appealing to the ambiguity of suffering and weakness. Unlike the unmistakable aroma of fresh baked apple pie, this fragrance is difficult to identify. Some will be convinced that it is the odor of decaying flesh; others will identify the odor as the fragrance of life. Both are correct. One recoils from the putrid stench of death; the other identifies incipient life in the same odor. The two aromas are so difficult to distinguish because one mingles with and rises from the other. Therefore, Paul's metaphor (or the rivals' metaphor applied to Paul) provokes the Corinthians to view God's work in weakness, vulnerability, and even failure. For although Paul's critics may think the odor hovering over Paul is the acrid stench of death, Paul invites his readers to understand the odor in quite a different manner. For those who believe, the odor is not the stench of death at all but the "aroma [*euodia*] of [the resurrected] Christ" (2:15).

In 2:17, Paul grows impatient with his metaphor, discarding it in favor of a frontal assault on his adversaries: "We are not peddlers of God's word like so many; but in Christ we [apostles] speak as persons of sincerity, as persons sent from God and standing in his presence" (my trans.). Ironically, the "hucksters" fail to see their own dishonesty, for their grandiose pretensions to life, success, and power are really nothing more than a massive denial of death. Moreover, their denial of death is a denial of Christ, because the brokenness and incompleteness of this world are no longer viewed in light of Paul's central metaphor, the death of Jesus. In saying, "We are the aroma of Christ" (2:15), clearly Paul felt pushed to the side by his critics, and with the margin came a powerful insight. Paul fastens on a metaphor that invites his readers to see new meaning in suffering, weakness, mortality, and even ineptitude. Such language effectually assumes the location and power to reassign marginal status and to invite his readers to examine his rivals' pretensions.

THE POT METAPHOR (4:7–18)

Two explicit references to the resurrection in 2 Corinthians (4:7–18 and 5:1–15) extend Paul's polemic. Furnish correctly notes that the point of 4:7–18 appears already in 4:7: "We have this treasure in clay jars."[15] In 4:1–6, Paul condemned those cunning missionaries who preach themselves (4:5), who tamper with God's word (4:2), and who are blind (4:4). In contrast to these arrogant and willful apostles with their disgraceful, underhanded tactics (4:2), Paul emphasizes that "this extraordinary power belongs to God and does not come from us" (4:7). Then he offers a trial list, a catalog (*peristaseis*) to underscore how fragile this mortal vessel is.[16] Compared to his charismastic rivals, who claimed that their physical presence radiated the presence of a powerful, glorious, resurrected Jesus, the homely pot is an apt metaphor for Paul's frail body and unimposing credentials. Paul offers his list of trials (4:8–10; cf. 6:4–10; 11:23–29; and 12:10) as an ironic counterpoint to their credentials—their visions, miracles, persuasive speech, and radiant glory. The list of his afflictions, persecutions, perplexities, and beatings (4:8–9), first mentioned in 1 Corinthians 4:10–13 and recalled later in Romans 8:35–39, details the way in which Paul participates in the death of Jesus. In this context, Paul likewise finds in the scars and bruises evidence that he is "always carrying in the body the death of Jesus" (4:10; see Gal. 6:17). The incarnation of life, Paul emphasizes, comes from the incarnation of death: "so that the life of Jesus may also be made visible in our bodies. For while we live, we are always being given up to death for Jesus' sake, so that the life of Jesus may be made visible in our mortal flesh" (4:10–11). This insistent linkage of death and life presses the radical critique begun in 2:14–17.

Like his critics, Paul envisions a successful resolution to the Jesus story, but it is a deferred resolution securely tied to the suffering Jesus. It allows no facile escape from either human frailty or the pain and frustration of mortality. Although the resolution is deferred, one can yet perceive its signs, hidden within human vulnerability and grief.

In 4:14–18, Paul ties the deferred resolution securely to the resurrection tradition that authenticates his apostleship and gospel: "because we know that the one who raised the Lord Jesus *will raise* us also with Jesus, and *will bring* us with you into his presence" (4:14). Also, Paul's critique of his rivals is based on the way that life, glory, and things eternal are carried in this vessel that the opponents dismiss as common and inconsequential. Paul agrees that his "outer nature is wasting away" and accepts this as a sign of weakness, but he disagrees with their assessment of human culpability. For although physical decay is progressive and terminal, neither for Paul nor for his addressees was it a mere natural process. It was a result of cosmic powers working upon us, as Sylvia Plath wrote, "stars grinding, crumb by crumb."[17] Nevertheless, even in the pain inflicted by these frosty perils, Paul claims the resurrection is anticipated even though not fully realized—"our inner nature is being renewed day by day" (4:16). Paul's radical response to the gospel of his competitors allowed for no appeal that was not framed by human frailty and mortality, by human history and worldliness. His gospel, of course, would strike his critics as a caricature of the glorious and triumphant experience they held out to discredit Paul and to entice support from his converts.

EARTHLY TENT AND HEAVENLY HOUSE
METAPHORS (5:1–15)

Although Paul's defense of his apostleship begun in 4:7 continues through 5:21, the liturgical use of 5:1–10 alone at funerals tends to confirm the unfortunate chapter division that has chapter 5 begin after 4:18. Moreover, the introduction of the tent metaphor in 5:1 predisposes one to view 5:1–10 in isolation from its context. In taking 5:1–10 to be an isolated unit, scholars tend to focus on the relevance of the tent, clothing, and nakedness metaphors for Paul's (changing?) view of the afterlife.[18] Allegedly, it was a narrow escape from death in Asia Minor shortly before that induced Paul to reevaluate his earlier conviction that he would be alive at Jesus' parousia (1 Thess. 4:17). This brush with death prompted Paul to reflect on the fate of the "spiritual body" between death and the end of the age. In other respects, Bultmann, followed by Schmithals, understood 5:1–5 to be a parenthetical polemic aimed at Gnostics, who looked forward to removing this world's garments. Paul's concern with clothing does seem to oppose a classical Gnostic understanding that associated salvation with the spirit's removal of the world' s clothing, including the body itself, thus freeing the unfettered spirit to ascend heavenward to share the divine fullness.[19]

Both of these views of 5:1–10, however, fail to account for the strong contextual ties between 5:1–10 and 4:16–18. Furnish shows how the contrasts beginning in 4:16 continue without interruption through 5:10.[20] The juxtaposition of "outer nature" with "inner nature," of momentary affliction with eternal glory, of what can be seen with what cannot be seen, and of the temporary with the eternal runs throughout. Opposites there include earthly tent/heavenly house; mortal-life; that known by faith/that known by visible forms (or sight); and outward appearance/what is in the heart. Contrary to Bultmann, therefore, 5:1–10 does not stand apart from its wider context as a polemical excursus but is part of Paul's response to the rivals to whom he has been reacting since the thanksgiving.

Three decades ago, Friedrich Lang correctly observed that 5:1–10 functions as a defense by Paul of his apostolic ministry and as a continuation of 4:16, which ends with a contrast in which Paul rebuts his rivals.[21] Identifying the earthly house with the heavenly, the rivals ignored the human limits and mortal weaknesses all people experience. Against Bultmann and Schmithals, Lang argued that 5:1–10 concerns itself less with future existence than with the way the kerygma addresses present existence. Paul devalues his competitors' glorification of the earthly house by calling it a tent and by removing it from earth to heaven, and he postpones occupation of the heavenly house to the future.[22] In contrast to those who live for themselves, Paul asserts that the "love of Christ urges us on" (himself and his coworkers, 5:14) and that love expressed itself in his death "for all," leading to an exhortation that believers "might live no longer for themselves [as do the false apostles], but for him who died and was raised for them" (5:15). Paul recognizes that the present life groans under its burden (5:3–4) and that

God has prepared us for this ordinary existence (5:5) rather than a glorious, ecstatic life. (Ralph Martin has also shown how Paul links ecstasy as a "gift of God" [5:13; 12:2–3] with a call "to serve the Lord in daily life" [5:9,10].)[23] Thus, association with the death and resurrection of Jesus brings concrete obligations for others.

In response to critics who claimed to be so alive with the glory of the risen Lord that they had overcome the yawning gulf between life in the divine and human worlds or between mortality and immortality, Paul reaffirmed the reality of the present separation. This bald recognition of the chasm between worlds aims to expose the emptiness of the rivals' claim to have overcome the alienation of cosmic dislocation. In a statement dripping with irony, Paul juxtaposes the handmade, earthly, destructible tent with the heavenly, eternal house not made with hands (5:1). As long as believers inhabit the earthly tent, they yearn to "be clothed" with the heavenly dwelling, and they groan under the burden of the alienation from that home (5:2). Bemoaning life in the earthly tent, they yearn not for nakedness (5:3) but to be further clothed so that the mortal will be swallowed up by life (5:4). In contrast with his opponents who claim to have overcome the distance between the human and divine worlds, Paul insists on a continuing cleavage. But even though the gulf of separation is formidable and painful, Paul grants that the separation is not total. For in the interim period God has given the Spirit to believers as a sign (*arrabōn*) of that life (5:5). Through the Spirit, the believer gains partial access to that life or a foretaste of the future glory or resurrected life. That preliminary and partial experience dulls but does not eradicate the pain of alienation. For so long as believers are at home in the body (*somati*) instead of in the tent (*skenous*), they remain separated from the Lord (5:6–10), making it necessary to walk by faith and not by visible forms (by which the rivals measure authentic life; 5:7). The believer's conduct in this world reflects the strength of that distant, sacred connection: "So whether we are at home or away, we make it our aim to please him" (5:9).

This special alienation informing 5:1–8 may reflect Hellenistic thinking and set the stage for the soaring excursus on reconciliation (5:16–21). But in 5:10, Paul abandons the spacial idiom for a standard piece of Christian apocalypticism: "For all of us must appear before the judgment seat of Christ, so that each may receive recompense for what has been done in the body, whether good or evil." This somber warning was aimed at the antagonists who challenged Paul's gospel and ridiculed his apostolicity. Against those who claimed that they had overcome the distance between the divine and the human and who argued that Paul's weakness indicated that he had not done so, Paul points to the gulf that remains. Against those who argued that Paul's frailty vitiated the integrity of his mission and that his appearance contradicted the true gospel and made him an imposter, Paul again points to the distance between the human and divine. Against those who saw themselves as having risen above human limits to unite with the Lord of glory, Paul calls attention to the dislocation and the pain that these limits inflict even on believers. To those who presumed to devalue Paul's apostleship and his gospel, Paul set himself and his critics, his work and theirs, before the coming judgment, and he did so because he was supremely confident that everything false in his rivals and their message would crumble while he and his gospel would be vindicated.

Fearing that his readers would point to his vigorous defense as boasting (5:12), Paul specifies the basis for his apostolic mission, namely, the "love of Christ" manifested in his death "for all" (5:14). As a result of Christ's death, "those who live" (i.e., believers) are to live "no longer for themselves." Paul condemns all those who "boast in outward appearance [literally, 'in the face'] and not in the heart" (5:12). He insists instead that the "love of Christ urges" believers on (5:14) to live "for him who died and was raised for them" (5:15). Here in the conclusion of this topical discussion appears the basis of Paul's theologizing. Against the claimants to a high level of spiritual immediacy, who misread human experience and falsify the gospel by severing the resurrection from the suffering and dying one, Paul points to the distance between life here and there, between now and then. In living "for him who died and was raised for them," however, they can, even while away from "home," affirm their tie to the other world, living for the dying and risen one and not for themselves. Yet following Jesus on this side of the divide provides no immediate escape from death's burden in all of its multiform expressions—human frailty, physical handicaps, declining strength in age, or lack of prowess or success—and living death in this world as an epiphany of the resurrected one is in no way synonymous with absolute alienation.

In 5:17–19, Paul appears to extend this motif:

> So if anyone is in Christ, there is a new creation: everything old has passed away; see, everything has become new! All this is from God, who reconciled us to himself through Christ, and has given us the ministry of reconciliation; that is, in Christ God was reconciling the world to himself, not counting their trespasses against them, and entrusting the message of reconciliation to us.

How is this poetic, perhaps creedal, affirmation related to Paul's polemic? Given his rivals' claim to have overcome the separation between the divine and the human worlds, Paul's magnificent prose about reconciliation would seem to affirm the gospel that he is contesting. This would be true had Paul not elsewhere made clear that the credo "God was in Christ" means "in Christ's death." Moreover, in passages bracketing this gospel summary, Paul shows that being a part of the new creation does not insulate one from the sober realities of this world (e.g., 5:4 and 6:2–5). In 6:2, after triumphantly declaring, "Behold, now is the day of salvation"—a statement that, if taken alone, would undercut his earlier polemic—Paul adds a list of trials associated with living in this *kairos*:

> [A]s servants of God we have commended ourselves in every way [as opposed to the way the rivals commend themselves]: through great endurance, in afflictions, hardships, calamities, beatings, imprisonments, riots, labors, sleepless nights, hunger. . . . We are treated as impostors, and

yet are true; as unknown, and yet are well known; *as dying, and see—we are alive; as punished, and yet not killed*; as sorrowful, yet always rejoicing; as poor, yet making many rich; as having nothing, and yet possessing everything. (6:4–10)

The words I have emphasized constitute Paul's last, and perhaps most apt, linkage of apostolic participation in Jesus' death and resurrection in 2 Corinthians. Here quite explicitly Paul finds that his own brutal experience parallels and participates symbolically in the death and resurrection of Jesus. Thus, Paul hopes to regain the confidence of his converts in Corinth who have become infatuated with, if not devotees of, a gospel validated with superficial and unambiguous proofs of success and grandeur. While his apostleship may have appeared to be a masochistic caricature to some and his gospel a perverse glorification of suffering to others, Paul hopes that his recollection of an essential feature of the gospel may still, in a world in which death was sometimes more real than life itself, provide some with a new way of understanding everyday existence that is more realistic than the sham gospel of the opponents. In their effort to push Paul to the margin and to discredit him fully, they have instead inspired a radical embrace of the human condition invaded by the divine in the human and dying Christ.

Paul's rivals in Corinth promised what everyone desires, namely, an immediate rescue from the one great absolute—death. By contrast, Paul's gospel spoke only of a future resurrection, coupled with a call to suffer with Christ in the present. Paul emphasized that part of the Jesus story that his rivals neglected and that part of the human experience that they tried to paper over. Although Paul's gospel offered no escape from the harsh realities of this world, it provided the flash of insight, the holy figure, and the historical event pregnant with meaning that made it possible to view those realities in a new way. In what others thought was the stench of death, Paul found the aroma of the resurrected Christ. Where others saw only mortality and the signs of death, Paul was able to exclaim, "Behold, we live." Thus, Paul's gospel of the death and resurrection of Jesus provided a means for discerning the true from the false—the true apostle from the huckster, the true witness from the imposter, true from trifling speech, true wealth from counterfeit coinage, and the true gospel from its glitzy rival focused on success and glory. For the confused and suspicious Corinthians, Paul sought to provide a canon by which to judge the validity of competing gospels and to discriminate between competing models of Christian life. When pushed to the margin or even beyond it by his rivals, he embraced the margin and turned it into a radical affirmation of the manifestation of the divine in this wonderfully complicated and even unfair human web beset by the grim realities of disease, famine, war, violence, pestilence, and death that seemed more real, more insistent, more immediate than life itself.

Chapter 5

Ambivalence and Ambiguity on the Margins

Oikoumenē *and the Limits of Pluralism*

Every child has experienced the pain of being excluded, and every child has suffered from being teased as different, weird, odd, or other.[1] Those childhood traumas unfortunately linger into adulthood, and also extend beyond individual to group experience. This chapter treats the tension between inclusion and exclusion in various Jewish Diaspora groups of the first century and of Paul and the early church in particular. Such groups, especially if they are minority or fringe groups, experience the pain of those realities on the margin. In this chapter, I explore the complexity of this life on the margin. Diaspora Judaism itself was a marginal expression. As a minority religious movement set in the midst of a powerful, alluring Hellenistic culture, Jews of the dispersion had a long history of coping with life on the margins. Most of the options considered here reveal a complex relationship between the majority and minority culture. Simplistic responses were largely eschewed, even though at one level they would have been enormously attractive. The aim here is to set Paul in this web of relationships with one added complication—his profound commitment to Jesus and his conviction that in Jesus' death and resurrection the final episode of history was being initiated. Yet, even in this Jewish messianist circle of certainty, uncertainties remained and tensions between competing worlds were enormous.

In the discussion below, I show how Paul's mission strategy was fraught with tension and ambiguity. The central question posed by this dynamic is how to respond to the outsider, the one who is different, and how to identify the limits of both exclusion and inclusion.

PLURALISM AND TEXTUAL INTERPRETATION

Once in a blue moon an essay appears that reshapes the discipline and permanently alters the way we think about Judaism in the ancient world. Such an essay by Nils Dahl showed how the convenient universalistic-particularistic dichotomy used to distinguish late Judaism from early Christianity was false.[2] Dahl showed first-century Judaism to be more universalistic than usually allowed and early Christianity to be more particularistic than normally recognized. While Dahl's position has become a scholarly consensus, more work is needed on the tensions between universalistic and particularistic tendencies in Diaspora Judaism and their possible influence on Paul. While Paul did not borrow directly from the Alexandrian community, that community provides a useful model, nevertheless, for understanding how Diaspora Jews balanced loyalty to the Jewish Torah, the temple, and the land with attraction to the Hellenistic culture. By sampling literature from that community, this chapter will deal with the tension between accommodation to and rejection of the Hellenistic culture within Alexandrian Jewry. We shall see how the community turned the symbols and rhetoric of the dominant culture to its own defense, and how the community embraced ecumenical tendencies while guarding its own particularity. By studying the ways the Diaspora community appropriated the Hellenistic vision of *oikoumenē* to lay claim to their status as God's elect, we may better understand how a Diaspora Jew like Paul could combine a universalistic Gentile mission with an appeal to a rather narrow slice of Jewish tradition.[3] I assume here that pluralism affects the way a community interprets its texts, and those texts then provide a lens through which the pluralistic setting is viewed. A clear grasp of this hermeneutical loop should give us a better understanding of the way Paul employed texts to develop a protocol for engaging the Hellenistic world.

THE SEPTUAGINT

A primary force shaping both the outlook of Paul and that of Alexandrian Judaism was the Septuagint (LXX). This translation did more than shape "outlook" in some general, vague sense; it provided a language for defining a world, as well as a protocol for crossing the margin and administering access. It provided the language, many of the models, and most of the sacred texts for Jewish writers from the third century to the first. Legends formed supporting its authoritative claim (e.g., the *Letter of Aristeas*).[4] Festivals arose celebrating its genesis and reinforcing its religious value. A vast body of commentary grew up linking it to the changing circumstances of the Jewish community in the Greco-Roman world. Aside from the works of figures such as Artapanus, Aristobulus, and Pseudo-Aristeas, most of the voluminous works of Philo either served as commentary on the LXX or appealed to it in the development of its argument.[5] These works show that among the vehicles of revelation, Philo assigned the preeminent place to the LXX.[6]

More than a text that generated interpretation, however, the text itself *was* an interpretation. Coming from different periods, from many hands, and written in the Hellenistic vernacular of the day,[7] the LXX was devoted to the exegesis of the Old Testament text as well as to its preservation in Greek.[8] While Georg Bertram noticed this tendency as early as 1936, no systematic study yet exists of the theological tendencies of the various books of the LXX.[9] Granting that the LXX was the Bible of Paul's Diaspora community and that it was in the blood of Paul himself,[10] such studies are a sine qua non for deciphering Paul's worldview. While a comprehensive treatment of the theological tendencies in the LXX is outside the scope of this paper, a consideration of the LXX of Isaiah is germane for our study of *oikoumenē* and the limits of pluralism.

Because of its ecumenical emphasis and its importance to Paul, our study must give Isaiah attention. Far from showing "obvious signs of incompetence," as Henry Barclay Swete charged,[11] the translation of Isaiah reflects a skillfully developed theological agenda. That agenda advocated the inclusion of Gentiles in the people of God and encouraged an expansion of *nomos* ("law") to include the language and ethos popular in circles of Hellenistic piety. The translators steered a middle course between strict and liberal interpretations, and sought to moderate tensions between traditions in conflict. When the LXX was translated, in the second century B.C.E. when relationships between the Seleucids and Palestinian Jewry were explosive, the translators of Isaiah emphasized the importance of constructive interaction with Gentiles. Their concern for the proselytes is evident in their emphasis on the universal reach of the Jewish religion. While they affirmed the importance of their Jewish tradition, they left open the possibility of a fruitful encounter with representatives of the Hellenistic world. The importance of this encounter is evident in their use of *oikoumenē* in the LXX of Isaiah.

Thirty-three of the fifty-four references to *oikoumenē* in the Old Testament appear in Isaiah and the Psalms (16 and 17 respectively). Only one anomalous reference appears in the entire Pentateuch (Exod. 16:35). Commonly used to refer to the whole inhabited world, *oikoumenē* usually renders the Hebrew words *tevel* and *eretz* but sometimes appears without warrant in the Hebrew text. Whereas Herodotus and Democritus used *oikoumenē* to refer to the civilized Greek world as opposed to the lands of the barbarians, Philo (who used the term fifty-seven times), like the Stoics and Cynics, expanded the scope of the term to embrace both Greeks and barbarians in the whole inhabited world.

While the LXX of Isaiah gives *oikoumenē* a dark as well as sunny side, announcing the Lord's stern judgment on all peoples (10:13; 13:9, 11), this divine condemnation was balanced by the promise of salvation for the *oikoumenē*. In

23:14–24:1, for example, the translator introduces salvation for peoples of the world into a Hebrew text. The Masoretic Text (MT) promises humiliation for Tyre: "The Lord will visit Tyre and she will return to her hire and will play the harlot with all the kingdoms of the world upon the face of the ground." This text universalizes sin and suffering rather than promise and consolation. The LXX, however, instead of this condemnation of Tyre for its historic association with the Canaanite fertility cult, promises redemption to Tyre: "The God of Tyre shall make a visitation and she will turn again to the old ways and shall be a port of merchandise for all the kingdoms of the world [*pasais tais basileiais tēs oikoumenēs*] and her merchandise and her hire shall be holy unto the Lord." Thus, the LXX reverses the indictment of Tyre appearing in the MT, and instead recognizes Tyre as the gateway through which eschatological benefits will flow from all the kingdoms of the world to Israel. Thus, the passage exchanges the humiliation predicted in the MT for a "holy" offering by the kingdoms of the world.

More dramatic, however, is the adaptation the LXX makes in the famous Zion poem in Isaiah 62. With an invocation of intensely personal if not erotic imagery, the MT places Zion securely at the center of Yahweh's affection:

> You shall no more be called *Azuvah* ["abandoned"],
> And your land shall no more be called *Shemamah* ["wasteland"],
> But you shall be called *Hephsi Bah* ["my delight is in her"]
> And your land *Be'ulah* ["mistress"]. (62:4)

This personal language is carried forward into verse 5b, where God as the bridegroom "rejoices over the bride."

In the LXX, however, the deeply personal or perhaps erotic nuances drop away, replaced by a Jewish piety that made Zion a symbol of habitation resonating with a wider meaning:

> And no longer shall you be called *Kataléleimmené* ["dismissed"],
> And your land shall no longer be called *Erēmos* ["desert"}],
> For you shall be called *Thelēma Emon* ["my will"],
> And your land *oikoumené*.

One could read *oikoumené* as a synonym of *gē* ("land" or "domesticated region"). Standing as an antithetical parallel to *erēmos* ("desert"), *oikoumené* might follow the Hebrew text promising human habitation for desolation. There are resonances, however, in the text itself that subvert that meaning. Two verses earlier in the LXX of 62:2, the *ethnē*, or peoples of the world, witness Zion's vindication and are joined by the kings of the world who give independent confirmation of Yahweh's righteous action. In the subtext, therefore, the Judaism of the text is able to read itself into the witness of the Gentiles. Were it not possible for the Jews of Alexandria to see themselves in the anomic world, Judaism would exist in total alienation. The terms with which the subtext embraces the "kings of the world" are quite clear. No longer will they dominate and exploit Zion. No longer will they feed themselves on her grain, nor slake their thirst with her wine (62:8).

Stripped of their status as superordinates, they will be discerning witnesses to the truth. Consequently, the text and subtext promise what Zion as *oikoumenē* will do, namely, provide an environment and a future in which tensions that dominate the relationship between Zion and the "nations" will be relaxed.

Those same tensions surely characterized the life of Diaspora Jews in Alexandria. Jews there sought direction for life in a setting in which they lived by Gentiles, traded with Gentiles, attended games and theater with Gentiles, and received education with and sometimes married Gentiles. The language, concepts, customs, practices, and piety that were inevitably absorbed from those associations were reconstructed by Jewish thinkers and refracted back onto the biblical text itself. Even when Jewish interests collided with those of their Gentile neighbors, the Hellenistic idiom remained integral to the Jewish identity. One such Hellenistic concept was *oikoumenē*.

There are signs within the LXX that these accommodations with Hellenistic universalism met resistance. The alarm expressed in 24:16 that Jews were abandoning *nomos* points to this conflict. Working off a Hebrew text which read, "Woe is me! For the treacherous deal treacherously; woe is me, for the treacherous deal treacherously," the translators made several alterations to address elements in the community whose attitudes toward the law were too liberal. Changing the object of the woe from *me* in the MT to *those*, the translators gave the redundant Hebrew a sharp twist: "Woe to those setting aside, those setting aside the law." This simple change made the text condemn those who were too casual about the specific requirements of *nomos* and the traditions it upheld.

Over forty years ago, I. L. Seeligmann noticed a condemnation of an anti-dogmatic faction in Isaiah 8:12–16.[12] He suggested that 8:11–14 lists the rhetoric and slogans of those who were indifferent to the study or observance of *nomos*. They accuse other Jews of being hard (*sklēron*, v. 12) and oppressive, and of requiring obedience to harsh, restrictive laws which ensnare their victims in a crippling bondage. This liberated faction urges other Jews to free themselves from superstitious allegiance to these laws and to worship the Lord in holiness and fear. By the clever addition of a conjunction, *dia touto* ("because" or "on account of this"), and a prepositional phrase, *en autois* ("among them"), in 8:15, the translator links the divine warning to ignore the errorists ("Do not call *sklēron* ['hard, harsh, austere'] everything that this people calls *sklēron*, and do not fear what they fear, nor be in dread") with the preceding threat ("on account of this [*dia touto*] many among them [*en autois*] will be powerless and will fall and be crushed; and those who are safe will draw near and be taken"). The translator added *tote* ("then"), linking this warning and prediction of judgment with 8:16: "Then [*tote*] those being sealed who do not teach the law will be manifest [*tote phaneroi esontai hooi sphragizomenoi ton nomontou memathein*]." The Greek of this passage bears little resemblance to the Hebrew command to "Bind up the testimony, seal the teaching among my disciples [*sor te'udah hathom torah belimudai*]." With these changes, the LXX had changed the warning of the MT against the strategy of political expediency invoked in the face of the Assyrian threat into an indictment of Jews who not only do not teach the law but actively oppose those observing the austere teachings of Torah. Conservatives and liberals were quarreling over the correct reading of the text. One faction called the other rigorist; the "rigorists" found their accusers guilty of apostasy for "setting aside" *nomos*. The disagreement was over the level of accommodation Jews could make with the Hellenistic environment and still remain Jews.

In some cases, the LXX was made to condemn the materialism of the dominant culture. The Hebrew of Isaiah 24:8, for example, identifies the exile as one of the darkest periods in Israel's history. The MT laments the despoiling of the land by the Babylonians, and blames lawlessness and covenant violation for this catastrophe (24:5). The description of the land's desolation is filled with pathos: "The wine mourns, the vine languishes" and "the roar of the jubilant has ceased." The LXX, however, rejects this political judgment in favor of other concerns: "The stubbornness and richness of the impious has ceased [*pepautai authadia kai ploutos asēbon*]" appears in place of "the roar of the jubilant has ceased." By substituting two words (*authadia* and *plutos* ["stubbornness" and "richness"]) for one (*sheon* [Heb., "roar"]) and identifying the offenders no longer as inhabitants in general but as *asēbon* ("impious") in particular, the translator recast the Hebrew to condemn behavior which Stoics and Cynics also found repugnant. This condemnation of atavistic greed only makes sense as a rejection of a very tempting option for Jews as well as Gentiles.

In spite of its obvious debt to Hellenistic culture, the Diaspora community often viewed itself as an island in a sea of *anomia* ("lawlessness"). Necessary for the definition of the Jewish community in Alexandria, *anomia* provided something for the community to push against. A devotion to *nomos* required its opposite to establish identity and to define piety.

In his study of the Psalms, Martin Flashar demonstrated how *anomia* expanded to refer to over twenty forbidden acts denounced in Hebrew.[13] He found *anomia* used for Hebrew terms such as *awon* ("sin"), *pasha'* ("apostasy"), *zad* ("arrogance"), *halal* ("boastfulness"), *rasha'* ("wickedness"), *hawah* ("crime"), and *awal* ("unrighteousness"). Reacting to this same tendency, the LXX of Isaiah used *anomia* for *pasha'* ("rebellion") six times,[14] *awon* ("iniquity") five times,[15] *hata* ("sin") two times,[16] and *awon* ("wickedness, trouble, sorrow") two times.[17] In single instances, *anomia* stands for a number of Hebrew words: *sarah* ("rebellion," 1:4); *mispach* ("bloodshed," 5:7); *rasha'* ("wickedness," 55:7); *ma'shakoth* ("fraudulent gain," 33:15), and *hamas* ("violence," 51:9). In 3:8 and 43:24, *anomia* appears in the text without justification from the Hebrew. Enjoying such a broad application, *anomia* was no anemic generalization but a canopy under which hovered a very broad range of misconduct not specifically condemned by the 613 commandments.

This identification of conduct outside the traditions of Israel as *anomia* and its condemnation contradicts the tendency, perhaps unconscious, to surrender to the allure of a powerful Hellenistic culture. On the one hand, both Hellenistic language and values intruded into the Jewish experience in Alexandria, yet on the other hand, the community viewed itself as an island in a sea of *anomia*. At one level the Jews were aware of being influenced, and yet at another level they repressed that awareness. So in this particular case the tension operated 'at a very deep level, and the tension operating at this unconscious level restrained pluralistic tendencies fostered by the spirit of *oikoumenē*. So a simple retrieval of the tradition was insufficient to maintain a sense of Jewish identity in Alexandria. The pluralism manifest in the Hellenistic world and the manifest ambiguity that created for the Jewish response could not be papered over with a simple division of the world into spheres of *anomia* and *nomos*. A new and more complex response was required from a community in which a metamorphosis was taking place.

In summary, the alterations surveyed here, some of them delicately nuanced and highly sophisticated, refute Swete's judgment that the LXX translation of Isaiah shows "obvious signs of incompetence." Instead, with sophistication and subtlety, the LXX of Isaiah altered the MT to stress theological issues of importance for the Alexandrian Jewish community. The universal emphasis admonished the community to be diligent about the inclusion and nurture of the *ethnē*. Along with this stress on inclusiveness went a *nomos* spirituality that absorbed into itself ideal elements of Hellenistic piety while simultaneously guarding against reckless compromises with the Hellenistic milieu. The mythic or symbolic interpretation of *nomos* not only offered protective benefits to the faithful but also provided a sacred connection with the heavenly realm and a prophylactic against excessive accommodation or *anomia*—a synonym of chaos and dislocation. So *oikoumenē* was informed by an understanding of *nomos* that allowed for the absorption of language, concepts, practices, and piety that were essentially Hellenistic yet guarded against absorption into the dominant culture. *Nomos* thus provided a way not only for penetrating and ordering chaos but also for balancing accommodation with the Hellenistic emphasis on *oikoumenē* with devotion to the ancestral religion. No mere legalistic system securing boundaries between Jew and Gentile (as Schoeps held was the case in Diaspora Judaism), *nomos* provided a protocol for crossing boundaries and interacting with neighbors who had become their cultural cohorts. Yet in this pluralistic setting, *nomos* did guard against extreme accommodations with the dominant culture without defining those accommodations precisely or in some cases without even bringing them to consciousness. And while the pluralism of the Diaspora affected the texts and the way they were read, the texts provided the lens through which the dominant Hellenistic culture was viewed, ordered, and subordinated. The stable ingredient in this strategy was tension between the affirmation of one's own tradition and a fruitful encounter with the dominant Hellenistic culture.

THE *LETTER OF ARISTEAS*

Noting the way Pseudo-Aristeas reaches out to the Hellenistic culture while clinging to his ancestral Jewish traditions, Victor Tcherikover concluded that

"Aristeas" sought to be a citizen of two worlds and succeeded in belonging to neither.[18] That Pseudo-Aristeas embraced the universalism of the Hellenistic world is generally recognized. The implied author shared the cosmopolitanism of King Ptolemy, whose love of the cultures of the world inspired his efforts to collect "all the books of the world [*oikoumenēn*]." (9). Our author notes that the tranquility of Ptolemy's kingdom and the esteem it enjoyed "throughout the inhabited world [*holen tēn oikoumenēn*]" prompted the king to dedicate "a thank-offering to God the Most High" (39). This Jewish commentator notes that the responses of the Jewish translators mirror this same cosmopolitanism. In responding to the king's question about piety, a Jew is made to say, "God is the benefactor of the whole world [*holon kosmon*]" (210). Another Jew advised the king to "practice benevolence to all men [*pantas anthropous*]" (225). And while looking to Jerusalem as an idealized source of Israel's scriptures and worship, Eleazar, the high priest, appears as a believer in God's universal rule, "every place being filled with his sovereignty [*plerōmenou pantos topou*]" (132). And even while condemning the "wisest of the Greeks" for their fabrication of images of wood and stone which they worship and the "very foolish . . . Egyptians," who worship beasts, serpents, and monsters (134–38), Pseudo-Aristeas encouraged tolerance as the *modus vivendi:* "Our law forbids harming anyone [*medena*] in thought or in deed," adding that the law encourages the extension of justice "to all humanity [*pros pantas anthrōpous*]" (168).

This cosmopolitanism carried with it a special piety and anthropology. We hear in Pseudo-Aristeas that the God of Israel is the same God all people worship, as the Gentiles say, "except that we have a different name. This name for him is Zeus and Jove. The primitive [peoples] consistently with this, demonstrated that the one by whom all live and are created is the master and Lord of all" (16). All humanity, we are told, respects the legislation of the Jews "concerning meat and drink" (128). The "letter" portrays King Ptolemy Philadelphus as one who recognizes and worships Israel's God and aims to promote "justice and piety in all things" (24). Moreover, the cultural ideal held up by "Aristeas" for all Jews to emulate comes from the Greek *paideia.* Their basic moral qualities are to include prudence (*sōphrosunē*), justice (*dikaiosunē*), temperance (*egkrateia*), and most especially moderation (*epieikēs*). And the ethical qualities they urge on the king are thoroughly Hellenistic—love of humanity (*philanthrōpia*), generosity (*epieikeia*), and magnanimity (*makrothumia*).[19] Moreover, the literary form and koine Greek of the letter itself reveal Hellenistic influence. The journey to Palestine follows patterns similar to those in utopian Greek novels, and the king's questions addressed to each of the seventy-two translators imitate the pattern of the Greek symposium.[20]

This document reveals that a real metamorphosis was taking place in the Jewish community in Alexandria. Even the representatives of Jerusalem appear as learned men who speak both Hebrew and Greek (121). Jewish dietary rules blend with Hellenistic wisdom. Jewish law and Hellenistic virtue coalesce. A significant number of the community concern themselves primarily with "eat, drink and pleasure" (223), and while the Sabbath law, circumcision, and prescriptions against eating pork went unchallenged, other dietary rules, the tefilin, and mesusot were neglected or ignored altogether.[21] Thus, we see that Hellenistic influence was pervasive and tended to weaken ties with what had historically been the primary symbols of Israel's faith, namely, the land, the temple, and even the covenant faith. So tolerance of the Greek neighbors and acceptance of their ways was at the expense of the ancestral religion.[22] As citizens of the *polis* became more cosmopolitan, ethnic identity eroded. Yet this erosion sparked off resistance. In a classic essay, Victor Tcherikover argued that the *Letter of Aristeas* was not written as propaganda to gain support from the Gentiles but to confirm the loyalty of Jews to traditions that were being eaten away.[23] But can that dialogue with insiders and propaganda aimed at outsiders be so neatly divorced? The integrity and identity of the community is often secured by rhetoric aimed at outsiders.[24] No internal dialogue can totally ignore one's relationship with outsiders, and no dialogue with the outsider can overlook the role of the insider. Tcherikover, nevertheless, held that in the *Letter of Aristeas* we find a conservative minority who were unable to free "themselves from the 'lack of education and stubbornness' of their Palestinian brothers . . . who continued to use the Hebrew Torah in spite of the fact that it was preserved in Alexandria only in bad copies."[25]

Tcherikover was correct to point out conflicting tendencies in the letter. Juxtaposed against liberalizing tendencies in the letter, reaffirmations of the power and importance of ancient symbols and rites appear. Contradicting the enthusiastic embrace of the language, literary forms, and philosophic views of the Hellenistic world seen in Pseudo-Aristeas's brief summary of the law (128–72) comes a divine mandate for the separation of Jews from Gentiles. Verses 139–40 especially insist on the separation of Jews from their "pagan" neighbors: "In his wisdom the legislator [Moses] . . . being endowed by God for the knowledge of universal truths, surrounded us with unbroken palisades of iron walls to prevent our mixing with any of the other peoples in any matter, being thus kept pure in body and soul, preserved from false beliefs, and worshiping the only God omnipotent over all creation."

How is one to understand these contradictory tendencies? Tcherikover located this duality in the situation of the Jewish community rather than the contradictions of "Aristeas." Turning against conservative Jews stubbornly clinging to a defective Hebrew Torah (30) and its flawed interpretation (144), Pseudo-Aristeas emphasized the advantages of a Greek education.[26] And against those conformist Jews, Pseudo-Aristeas insists on the laws and customs that separate Jews and Gentiles. It was this strategy that caused Tcherikover to observe that Pseudo-Aristeas was a citizen of two worlds but belonged to neither. But Tcherikover's solution is too extreme and leaves the internal contradictions unresolved.

J. J. Collins argues that the contradictions come from the attempt by Pseudo-Aristeas to address two different audiences. He sought to reassure Gentiles of Jewish trustworthiness and fidelity to Ptolemaic interests, and at the same time he hoped to confirm Jews in their faithfulness to their traditions that distinguished them from Gentiles.[27]

Rather than concentrating on the audiences, it might be more useful to concentrate on the high level of ambiguity created by the metamorphosis taking place in a community on the margin. That ambiguity is evident in the letter in the emerging conflict between the nostalgia for the coherent religious world of shared meaning represented by the temple and high priest (but without reference to sacrifice!) and powerful pluralistic tendencies of a vibrant, alluring Hellenistic culture. While earnest, pious Jews in Alexandria knew cultural alienation, Jews at home in the discourse of the Hellenistic world experienced religious alienation. This work is hardly about the divorce of those worlds, however, but about their coexistence within the community itself and the ability of Jews to live with the resulting ambiguity. Consequently, Pseudo-Aristeas's interpretation of the nature and function of law viewed the law as an instrument for mediating but not resolving the tension. He found confirmation for the authority of the law in the Hellenistic world itself, with the independent recognition by the king of "your law" (32). King Philadelphus is summoned by Pseudo-Aristeas to pay homage to the law as the very *logia theou* (177, 179), and even Greek poets and writers appear in the letter offering testimonials to the sacred character of Torah (31). Thus, ironically, Pseudo-Aristeas found in the cosmopolitan Hellenistic culture itself support for placing limits on pluralism.

The central significance of the law for the Diaspora community was hardly in question, but a fresh interpretation of the law was required by the sophisticated, urban Hellenistic milieu framing Alexandrian Judaism. The condemnation of idol worship (135–38) and the allegorical interpretation of the laws of purity would have offended no member of the Hellenistic intelligentsia. Pseudo-Aristeas thus offered a common meeting ground for both serious, inquiring Jews and Gentiles. But he did more. He provided a corrective for those tempted to abandon the law altogether in the pursuit of "eat, drink and pleasure"(223). Thus, we see that it was the interpretation, not the translation, that was of primary importance to Aristeas (15). The combination of his commentary on law observance and his stress on the classic Hellenistic virtues was not without tension.[28] Pseudo-Aristeas strained to be a citizen of both worlds. He sought a way, as did the LXX of Isaiah, to remain loyal to the ancestral Jewish traditions while remaining open to the surprises and fruits of the Hellenistic encounter. The tensions in the narrative reflect the tensions of his situation, tensions that were to remain unresolved for some centuries to come. But what is distinctive about Pseudo-Aristeas's vision of *oikoumenē* is the high level of ambiguity he allows in the enormously complex interaction of a Jewish community in a pluralistic setting. In short, ambiguity was recognized as a given of life at the margin.

PHILO

In a rare personal outburst, Philo opens book 3 of the *Special Laws* with an outpouring of devotion to his two great loves—the Pentateuch and philosophy:

> There was a time when I had leisure for philosophy and for contemplation of the universe and its contents, when I made its spirit my own in all its beauty and loveliness and true blessedness, when my constant companions were divine themes and verities wherein I rejoiced with a joy that never cloyed or sated. (3.1)

Kept from his beloved studies by "civil cares," Philo, nevertheless, kept alive in his soul "the yearning for culture which . . . lifts me up and relieves my pain" (3.4). Thus, Philo was emboldened not only to "read the sacred messages of Moses, but also in my love and knowledge to peer into each of them and unfold and reveal what is not known to the multitudes" (3.6). This philosophical lens through which Philo read "Moses" goes far to explain the tension between his understanding of *oikoumenē,* a Hellenistic creation, and his ancestral religion.

Although Philo employed a rich vocabulary to express his universalistic outlook, one of the most important words in that vocabulary was *oikoumenē.* Given the Stoic and Cynic influence on Philo, the frequent appearance of *oikoumenē* in his writings (fifty-seven times) comes as no surprise. Nevertheless, in his use of *oikoumenē* as in that of Pseudo-Aristeas, ambiguity abounds. Certainly Philo recognized the importance of the *polis* and its laws for both Jews and Greeks. At one level, as a Jew Philo was at home with the idiom and ways of his Hellenistic habitat. Yet he found in the Stoic view of the world as a cosmopolis a critique of the traditional *polis* that well suited his marginal status as a Diaspora Jew. Appealing to this Stoic concept, Philo went beyond the biblical text to claim citizenship in a world *polis* ruled by a single law and polity: "For this world is the Megalopolis or 'great city,' and it has a single polity and a single law, and this is the word or reason of nature [*logos physeōs*]" (*Joseph* 29). Elsewhere, he noted the harmony of the law with the world and the world with the law that makes the observer of the law a "loyal citizen of the world [*kosmopolitou*]" (*Creation* 3; also *Abraham* 61).[29] Everywhere, equally uniform and valid, loyalty to this law transcended one's duty to any particular *polis.*

In Moses 1.156–57, Philo offers his most cogent summary of this universalism. Referring to Moses, Philo says,

> Each element obeyed him as its master, changed its natural properties and submitted to his command, and this perhaps is no wonder. For if, as the proverb says, what belongs to friends is common, and the prophet is called the friend of God, it would follow that he shares also God's possessions, so far as it is serviceable. For God possesses all things, but needs nothing; while the good man, though he possess nothing in the proper sense, not even himself, partakes of the precious things of God so far as he is capable. And that is but natural, for he is a world citizen [*kosmopolitēs*], and therefore not on the roll of any city of the human habitations of the world [*oudemia tōn kata tēn oikoumenēn poleōn enegraphē*], rightly so because he has received no mere piece of land but the whole world as his portion [*holon ton kosmon klēron labōn*].

In addition to Moses, Philo spoke of Adam, Abraham, and all the wise as citizens of the world (*kosmopolitēn; Creation* 142): "Now the world of the wise man, the world citizen [*ho cosmopolitēs sophos*], is filled full of good things many and great, but the remaining mass of men experiences evil things in greater number, but fewer good things" (*Migration* 59). And he extended world citizenship (*kosmopolitidēs*) to all those who consecrate themselves as an offering to God, from which no mortal attraction dissuades them (*Dreams* 1.243). While the citizenship in the cosmos had a vertical dimension, Philo extended it horizontally to embrace the whole of the inhabited world (*Joseph* 21). This view of the Hellenistic world was informed by a vital biblical tradition to which he appealed for support, but inevitably tensions arose when that tradition collided with the politics of Hellenistic cities. Drawing on his understanding of Septuagintal law, he condemned the covetous designs of the fractured and contradictory laws of various cities (*Joseph* 30) that were nothing more than human addenda to the "single polity of nature" (*Joseph* 31). And he drew an unfavorable contrast between Jewish solidarity and Greek and barbarian factiousness. That children shared the fate of traitors he called repulsive, and that a poll tax was levied not on property but on bodies he criticized as uncivilized and devoid of "humane culture" (*Spec. Laws* 3.163–64). Unlike the laws of Rome, Philo had Moses propose swift justice for prisoners lest the offender multiply the crime (*Spec. Laws* 3.102). He detested Solon's practice of permitting marriage with "half sisters" on the father's side,[30] and the Egyptian permission of marriage with sisters on both sides of the family.[31] He condemned the Spartans as too austere and the Ionians too lax. By contrast, Moses followed the golden mean, relaxing the overly strict laws and tightening the loose, and thus achieving "harmony and concord" (*Spec. Laws* 4.102). According to Philo, when Moses forbade the consumption of meat from animals dying naturally or being killed by beasts, he repudiated the practice of skillful, aristocratic Greek hunters who bagged their game and parceled it out in an act of generosity (*Spec. Laws* 4.120). Finally, he applauded the "holy Moses" for condemning child sacrifice and the burning of sons and daughters as an abomination and a dastardly, polluting deed (*Abraham* 181). This stark contrast between Jewish and Hellenistic polity he used to emphasize the superiority of Mosaic law. Nevertheless, his description of Mosaic law as a perfect copy of the invisible, eternal, divine, natural law depends on Hellenistic concepts. Furthermore, his description of the true *cosmopolitēs* as the observer of the Mosaic law links Jewish tradition and Hellenistic culture. So even in differentiating Jewish and Hellenistic ways, Philo forged links between them.

In this uneasy coupling of the two traditions, the emphasis was not always balanced. Because of the weak position of the Jewish community in a dominant culture, the greater risk was excessive conformity to the Hellenistic culture. Without declining its nature, Philo repeatedly warned his people of the evils of apostasy.[32] But he sharply criticized rigorist Jewish conservatives as well. He condemned scriptural literalists as "slow witted" (*Flight* 179; *Dreams* 1.39), "obstinate," "rigid," and "resentful" (*Dreams* 2.301), and accused them of rejecting the truth of the Scriptures and even of apostasy (*Confusion* 2.6–8; *Agriculture* 157). He simultaneously repudiated symbolic and intellectual readings of *nomos* that

treated the literal sense of *nomos* with "easy going neglect." He rejected a spirituality that so elevated "what is not seen" that it eclipsed "what is seen" in the text.
He castigated Jews who neglected the letter of the law, arguing that "they ought
to have given careful attention to both aims, to a more full and exact investiga-
tion of what is not seen and to a blameless stewardship of what is seen" (*Migration* 89–94). As he scolded sophisticated, conformist Jews, and chided rigorist
Jews obsessed with the literal message of texts, he aimed to steer a middle course
between the two. That middle course was inevitably steadfastly held by tension
between the extremes. Given Philo's own sophistication and the ease with which
he moved in Hellenistic circles, his condemnation of other Jewish sophisticates
may sound hollow or even hypocritical unless one realizes that these condemna-
tions reflect the tensions within Philo's own soul.

The need for Philo to defend proselytes from discrimination within the Jewish community itself and his simultaneous endorsement of Hellenistic philosophy may indicate the level of tension within the community itself. Only the
fruitful interaction between Judaism and Hellenism would protect the Jewish
community from total alienation or complete assimilation. One way Philo
escaped alienation was by incorporating the great philosophers into the traditions
of Israel. By making Moses the source of their genius, he was able to see Judaism's
self in the other, and rejection of that world inevitably would mean self-rejection.
Equally important, however, was Philo's concern for the welfare of the proselyte.
That proselytes participated in the life of the Jewish community is clear, but their
status was ambiguous.[33] By identifying the Israelites themselves as proselytes and
recipients of God's gift and promise, Philo elevated the status of the proselytes in
his own community (*Cherubim* 108; *Dreams* 2.272–73; *Spec. Laws* 1.308). By
exhorting the community to accept and encourage proselytes, Philo was asking
the marginalized not to marginalize others in turn. When Gentiles married to
Jewish men were diminished, Philo cited with approval Moses' decision to allow
Hebrew fugitives from Egypt to keep their Egyptian wives. In reconciling Jews
and Gentiles within the community, Philo's *oikoumenē* received a very immediate relevance.[34] In *On the Special Laws* 1.51–52, Philo embraces the proselytes
with a special tenderness:

> [T]hey have left . . . their country, their kinsfolk and their friends for the
> sake of virtue and religion. Let them not be denied another citizenship or
> other ties of family and friendship, and let them find places of shelter stand-
> ing ready for refugees to the camp of piety. For the most effectual love-
> charm, the chain which binds indissolubly the goodwill which makes us one
> is to honor the one God.

Had the community not felt attenuated by the proselyte presence, such an exhortation would have been unnecessary. Although Philo knew that observance of the
Jewish religion sometimes brought one into conflict with the Gentiles in the *polis*,
he insisted that Jews embrace believing Gentiles. Philo's aim was, as Tcherikover
noted, to allow the Jew to remain a Jew and, at the same time, to belong to the

elect society of the Greeks, the bearers of world culture.[35] Yet this synthesis was always being tested by centrifugal forces from within and centripetal forces from without.

We see, therefore, that in Philo, as in Pseudo-Aristeas and the LXX of Isaiah, tension was the norm. The obligations of membership in the *polis* often clashed with the claims of citizenship in the megalopolis. And defining a *cosmopolitēs* as a person made wise by a deep understanding of the Scriptures placed Jews at odds with Hellenistic conventions. Jews easily swayed by the claims of the dominant culture quarreled with members of the Diaspora who were more hostile to Hellenism. The conflict without was matched by a struggle within as the individual debated the wisdom of a cosmopolitanism that undermined Jewish identity. Twin forms of alienation were the Scylla and Charybdis of Alexandrian Jews. According to Philo, only a steady course between these twin perils could save the community from being devoured by the dominant culture and a consequent alienation from one's Jewishness or being wrecked by total withdrawal into a cultural ghetto and alienation from the dominant culture. To guard that balance was an important part of the task of Philo, Pseudo-Aristeas, and even the LXX of Isaiah.

PAUL

R. J. Z. Werblowsky maintains that the portrayal of Paul as a "typical 'Dispersion Jew' is sheer nonsense."[36] Given Paul's upbringing in the Diaspora, his Diaspora Bible (the LXX), his Greek language, and his education in the Diaspora, one must respond that a consideration of Paul that does not take account of the influence of the Diaspora on his theology is nonsense. Some such connection was suggested by Nils Dahl in his commentary on Romans 3:29–30: "In drawing the consequence that radical monotheism excludes any distinction [i.e., between Jew and Gentile], Paul shows some affinity with Greek philosophical monotheism, which was universalistic and more or less cosmopolitan. Since Xenophanes, it could include polemic against religious particularism."[37] Dahl believes such influences were mediated by a Hellenized Judaism that used them for apologetic purposes "to prove the excellency of the Mosaic legislation and of the Jewish nation."[38] Our presentation focuses on the contradictory impulses within the Diaspora community, and on the unresolved tensions between *oikoumenē* and particularism within that circle. If we take Paul's Diaspora experience seriously, the question inevitably rises whether those same tensions characterized Paul's outlook, and if so to what extent.

Oikoumenē appears only once in Paul's letters and then only in a citation from the LXX of the Psalms.[39] That single appearance, however, comes at a critical juncture in Paul's argument. In a justification of the gospel mission that sounds quite autobiographical, Paul uses Psalm 19:4 to frame his rhetorical question in Romans 10:18: "Have they [the Gentiles] not heard?" He answers the question with a citation from the Psalms:

> Their voice has gone out to all the earth,
>   and their words to the ends of the world [*eis ta perata tēs oik-
>   oumenēs*].

Then Paul observes (not questions, as in the NRSV): "Again, I say, Israel did not understand" (10:19). But Paul is soon to insist from different points of view that the inclusion of the Gentiles or the *oikoumenē* does not mean either that God has rejected his chosen (11:1) or that Israel has stumbled so as to fall (11:11).

Of course, as F. Mussner has shown, the economical use of the word *oikoumenē* hardly means that Paul's universal perspective is inconsequential.[40] As Lloyd Gaston has successfully argued, the *pas* or "all" vocabulary in Romans is "inclusive language" that shows how self-consciously ecumenical Paul's thinking really was.[41]

We have space to note only briefly the enormous tension between Paul's kerygma for the *oikoumenē* and his pledge of loyalty to Israel in Romans 9–11. Paul stands on the boundary between Israel and the Gentiles. The stress of living on the boundary resembles the tension between boundlessness and boundedness that Victor Turner believes is characteristic of the liminal stage of myth and ritual. Following the mythic structure developed by Arnold van Gennep of rites of passage,[42] Turner shows how in the liminal stage tensions are created by competing tendencies—a straining toward universalization (or boundlessness) and a desire to impose structure (or limit, or boundedness) on the surge toward universalization.[43] Such a model aptly characterizes Paul's position and tendency. As we have noted, Paul's apocalypticism placed him in a liminal stage or transitional phase which allowed him to go beyond the Alexandrian community in his embrace of "Gentile sinners" while defending his loyalty to the ancestral religion of the Jews. For who has known the mind of the Lord?

At one end of the spectrum, but still within the circle of the ancestral faith, Paul argued that God will include Gentiles of the *oikoumenē* while remaining faithful to Israel. Thus, his dialogue with the synagogue was complicated by inclusive tendencies set loose by his gospel. And while the limit of pluralism for Philo was where *nomos* and *anomia* collided, the limit for Paul was quite different. Paul's eschatology dictated a revaluation of *nomos*. The messianic age that Paul inhabited in Christ encouraged a dramatic revision of Torah: Christ became Abraham's seed (singular, Gal. 3:15); through faith Abraham became the forefather of many Gentiles (Rom. 4:17); and Christ became the goal (*telos*) of the law (Rom. 10:4). Paul himself claims to be *en nomos Christou* (1 Cor. 9:21) to win those "outside the law" (i.e., Gentiles, 1 Cor. 9:21). In Romans 8:2, the "law of the spirit [*nomos tou pneumatos*] of the life in Christ Jesus" is a prescription to set free from the *nomos tēs hamartias kai tou thanatou*, which I take to refer to the "principle of sin and death." And the life now lived in *dikaiosunē* was seen as the antithesis of the life once lived in *anomia* (Rom. 6:19).[44] Paul still belongs somewhere on the spectrum of Diaspora Judaism, though his apocalyptic tendencies admittedly place him at one end of the spectrum. His messianism may have pushed him toward a more radical vision of the *oikoumenē* and the role of the Gentiles in the people of God than was possible in Alexandrian Judaism. But Paul's radical monotheism that eliminated any distinction between Jews and Gentiles shows "some affinity with Greek philosophical monotheism, which was universalistic and more or less cosmopolitan."[45] Nevertheless, Paul argues that he still belongs within the circle of faith drawn by God's covenant with Israel (2 Cor. 11:22–23). Thus, we see that tension between universalism and particularism was present in both the Alexandrian and Pauline writings; the difference between them was one of degree, not of kind. If my suggestion is correct, the Alexandrian exemplar may offer a useful model for understanding both the nature of those tensions and the way they were mediated in the Pauline letters. Far from being sheer nonsense, the assessment of Paul's place in Diaspora Judaism may be crucial to understanding the dynamic of his theology.

Chapter 6

The Grammar of Election

A Theology Negotiated at the Margins

I suspect that the majority of Pauline scholars hold the view that Paul began his apostolic ministry with a set of core beliefs that remained the same throughout his ministry. Whether this time of full awareness began at his "conversion" or was hammered out during the silent years in Arabia, the end result was the same: Convictions that appear either in the text or subtext of the letters remain remarkably stable from the first letter to the last. Such a view of Paul posits a theology integrated around an unshakable set of beliefs or truths serving as the organizing principle for Paul's theology. It certainly is the case that Paul did not come to the composition of the letters theologically naked. As a zealous Israelite, he would have simply taken for granted certain deep theological convictions even when he felt no need to justify them. They would have been encoded in the scriptures he knew, the story of Israel that he inhabited, and even in the theological grammar and syntax that were second nature to him. His view of God as creator and redeemer, as sovereign and free, as judge who condemns sin and lifts up the lowly, and as the one who chose Israel as his beloved and remained faithful to the covenant established with her, all had deep roots in Paul's ancestral faith. His confidence in God as the one who acts and will bring the human story to a positive end with the vindication of the chosen was surely a conviction that Paul carried

with him into his devotion to Messiah Jesus. Many, perhaps most, Pauline scholars would argue that this internal consistency that characterized Paul before his
"conversion" also aptly describes his life as an apostle from beginning to end.
After this singular moment and after his time in Arabia and his life in the church,
he began his apostolic ministry with a high level of certainty about the meaning
of such important theological concepts as election and covenant, and that conviction remained unaltered until the end of his life. Ironically, such scholars
might see less variety in Paul's view of election than in the constructions found
in the Hebrew Bible by the Yahwist, or the Deuteronomist, or prophets like
Hosea and Ezekiel, or even in the views of the Dead Sea "sectarians."

My thesis here is different. I hold no less than most that the epiphany of the
risen Christ for Paul was a dramatic, life-altering event, and that through his recognition of Jesus as Messiah and his call to be an apostle to the Gentiles he was, he
believed, set on the cosmic stage on which the final eschatological scene was being
played out. At the same time, I suggest that while Paul's thinking about election
was informed by a rich and venerable tradition and by his experience of Christ, it
was in his ad hoc responses to his context and that of his churches that he was
required to think through the implications of his version of the gospel to the Gentiles for the scriptural view of election. Even while his thinking was shaped by the
story of Israel that he inhabited and by the traditions about Messiah Jesus that he
had lately come to know, his collision with new challenges required fresh theological thinking. In those encounters we see novel combinations, new interpretive
schemes, daring innovations, exciting improvisations, and even heroic struggles to
work through troubling issues waiting to be settled or even to remain unsettled. I
am eager to capture some of the humanity of Paul who, like us, often did not know
what he thought about a given issue until he was forced by a challenge. The portrait of him as a theological colossus governed by a consistent and even systematic
theology is a post facto creation. The Paul of the letters was something else
entirely—a person bedeviled by doubts and anxiety, troubled by false charges and
slander, and distressed by the painful memory of his persecution of the church and
by the rejection of Jesus as Messiah by most of his kin. In this chapter I will
attempt to show how this Paul in his encounters with concrete realities shaped a
multifaceted view of election that included Gentiles even while affirming the
validity of God's promises to Israel. This task was dictated by his conviction that
God set him on the margin between intersecting ages where he was to serve as a
liminal figure. The tensions between inclusion and exclusion are almost palpable,
with Paul's resolution coming near the end of his apostolic ministry. And even
then, as we shall later see, that resolution had tragedy embedded within it. His
view of election came less though a routine evolutionary process that was always
directed in an upward, straight trajectory than through fierce, even heated,
exchanges. His theology of election, thus, is better called an emergent theology
than a core value, definable and even rather static. In this chapter I shall try to
trace Paul's emergent theology of election by attending to the grammar of election
in selected letters.

THE GRAMMAR OF ELECTION

The word *grammar* carries at least three meanings: First, it can refer to the rules by which subjects, objects, verbs, predicate adjectives, and other parts of speech relate to each other in a sentence. Second, it can signify the basic principles of the arts or sciences. For the past two centuries the word has been used in this manner, referring variously to a "grammar of assent," a "grammar of painting," a "grammar of ancient geography," a "grammar of music," and, more recently, a "grammar of film."[1] Third, as philosophers of language have shown, it can also refer to the way language, symbols, metaphors, cultic acts, and myths collaborate to shape a community's identity, its view of reality, its world construction, and its interaction with its context. A study of grammar in this sense is concerned with the way language *shapes* rather than merely *expresses* one's view of the world. It is in this latter sense that I use the term *grammar* here. In using the phrase *grammar of election* in this third sense, I am obviously relying on Wittgenstein and following theologians such as George A. Lindbeck, Wayne Proudfoot, D. Z. Phillips, and Paul Holmer, who speak of a "grammar of faith" as an alternative to the foundational approach to theology.[2] So far, however, the insights of these theologians have received scant attention from New Testament scholars. Given the frustrating attempts to find a center of Pauline theology, this latter approach may have special relevance for our discussion.

In his treatment of theology as grammar, Wittgenstein suggested, *"essence* is expressed by grammar" rather than the reverse—at least in a primary sense.[3] By this Wittgenstein meant that *essence* is not known as an independent entity in space but rather is apprehended through language. Even colors, he noted, are learned not through their separate independent existence, but through language. Under promptings from parents, teachers, siblings, and friends who point to a color saying, "See! This is red," children learn their colors. He noted with satisfaction that color recognition is a linguistic phenomenon. For example, the color turquoise is known and experienced through language, and cultures without words for turquoise do not recognize the color. From this experience comes an interest in the way this color fits and works together with other hues—pink, brown, yellow, black, chartreuse, and so forth—to form patterns, contrasts, and various cultural expressions. The way these fit and work together is their grammar. Inasmuch as the way things fit and work together is context-sensitive, Wittgenstein called this grammar "a language game," with its own rules, parts, actions, and goals. Even the parts that fit together function differently from game to game (in Paul's case, from letter to letter?). The queen of spades, for example, means one thing in a game of hearts and quite another in a game of bridge. Dice function differently in Monopoly, Trivial Pursuit, and craps. The mistake made by theologians, according to Wittgenstein, is that they focus on the *form* of expressions and not on their *use* or their context (i.e., the game in which they are used). The word *game* as Wittgenstein used it need not carry a pejorative or trivial sense but should suggest another way of looking at the rules of discourse Paul follows in different letters as he does theology. Observing this process is giving attention to the grammar of election.

George Lindbeck's adoption of elements of Wittgenstein's approach is instructive. Under the heading "Grammar and Doctrine, Continuity and Change," Lindbeck has explicitly noted that doctrine reflects the grammar of theology.[4] If one were to try to state what is absolutely basic for Paul, might it not be God? Were that the case, one would hardly be closer to understanding Paul's theology. According to Lindbeck, one would still need to determine what the word *God* meant for Paul, and one would learn that meaning by examining "how the word operates within [Paul's] religion and hereby shapes reality and experience rather than by first establishing its propositional or experiential meaning and reinterpreting or reformulating its use accordingly."[5]

By focusing on grammar, Wittgenstein and Lindbeck encourage us to look at all aspects of language in its human web—namely, symbols, actions, metaphors, and the way they fit together. We learn about one part of a web not by concentrating on the essence of that constituent element or even by isolating each element for examination but by observing how it works or fits with its other parts and context. This approach has at least two implications for our study of election in the Pauline letters. First, it suggests that we focus not so much on what the text signifies in a propositional or foundational sense as on how election operates in the text to direct the community. The term *election* in the Hebrew Bible is an old symbol often referring to the choice of Israel as God's beloved. Even there, however, scholars note the different ways the Yahwist, Deuteronomist, Hosea, Ezekiel, and the Qumran sectarians understand election. It is insufficient, therefore, simply to note that Paul inherited the term and used it. We must note how Paul's thinking was shaped by this venerable and varied tradition, and how his context required fresh thinking about the tradition. In his specific response to his context, the term *election* will likely acquire new meaning for Paul. The second implication of focusing on grammar in this study is that attention must be given to the way the term *election* fits into a larger language field and the way that field fits in its epistolary context. By looking at the larger interpretative scheme, we witness Paul's composition of fresh combinations, his new thinking, and his innovation. Even while his thinking is shaped by such a storied tradition, his collision with new contrarieties opens the way to new theological formulations. The study of this process may give us a more reliable basis for guessing at the meaning of Paul's theologizing about election in the letters discussed below.

1 THESSALONIANS

Context of Paul's Grammar of Election

The situation of the Thessalonians is hardly transparent. Even granting that Paul's letter may suppress conflicting voices and opinions, may mask skepticism about his gospel, and may conceal ambivalence in the community, some things are obvious, nevertheless. First, believers were suffering for their association with Christ (1:4–6; 2:13–16; 3:3–4). Some baptized members of the church had died, but we cannot be certain if they had been murdered by enemies or had died of natural causes. In any case, discouragement bordering on despair is implied by Paul's strong contrary emphasis on hope and steadfastness (1:3; 2:19; 4:13; 5:8). Second, although the danger of backsliding was real, we cannot be certain that Paul's exhortation to "abstain from immorality" (my translation of 4:3) was provoked by eschatological enthusiasm, the allure of Hellenistic religion, or persecution. In spite of these uncertainties, his warnings against pollution and erection of discrete boundaries between the insiders and outsiders do suggest a level of ambiguity that threatened the health, if not existence, of the community (e.g., 4:5). Third, there was some problem with the disorderly that caused Paul to encourage their correction (5:14). Although the disorderly (*ataktoi*) have been identified with the God-taught (*theodidaktoi*, 4:9) who have quit work to wait for Jesus' coming (*parousia*),[6] certainty about their identity eludes us. For whatever reason, the disorderly or idle posed problems Paul recognized and presumably sought to address.

Paul's Language of Election

Outside of Romans, Paul uses the word "election" (*eklogē*) only in 1 Thessalonians 1:4, referring to "brothers and sisters beloved by God, your election." Synonymous with this warm, familial language referring to God's election, Paul uses "call" (*kaleo*) in a dual sense—referring to God's election of a people and to the status of that people as God's elect (2:12; 4:7; 5:24). Paul rarely uses *etheto* (aorist middle of *tithēmi*), meaning to appoint or destine a people for salvation (5:9). The richness and diversity of Paul's language about the identity of God's elite are masked from us by its familiarity. Some of that language is traditional (church, *ekklesia*; saints, *hagioi*; father, *pater*; brothers, *adelphoi* [1:1; 3:13; 3:11; 2:14]), and some is freshly minted, referring to those in Christ (*en Christo*), in the Lord (*en kurio*), in God (*en theo*), and the God-taught (*theodidaktoi*) (1:1; 4:16; 3:3; 5:18; 4:9). This language distinguishes them from pagan Gentiles (*ta ethnē*), who, as they once did, worship "dumb idols" (1:9).

Given the presence of traditional language referring to God's elite, the absence of a single reference to the community of Israel in this letter is amazing.[7] This omission poses a challenge for those who believe that the covenant community of Israel stands at the center of Paul's theology. Not only are there no references to Israel in 1 Thessalonians; there are also no citations from the Hebrew Scriptures, no allusions to God's covenant or Torah or law (*nomos*), and no appeal to God's historic promises to Israel. Surprisingly, the cascade of apocalyptic metaphors in 4:13–5:11 nowhere touches the experience of Israel, even though the language itself has a Jewish provenance. These omissions are especially puzzling in light of Paul's use of the term *ekklesia* ("church" or "assembly") to name the elect community without any acknowledgment of its association with the *ekklēsia kuriou* ("assembly of the Lord") of the Septuagint (Deut. 23:2; 1 Chron. 28:8; Neh. 13:1; Mic. 2:5; etc.). Nowhere does Paul hint at the way this assembly of Gentiles was grafted onto God's holy tree, Israel. Except for one fleeting reference to the prophets, the history of this community has its beginning with Jesus' word and death in the recent past and will find its resolution in Paul's own lifetime. This extreme foreshortening, so common in Jewish apocalyptic writings, may help explain this Pauline truncation, but if Paul's theology is in its early formative stages, the difficult questions about the relationship of the *ekklēsia* of the Gentiles to the *ekklēsia* of Israel had not yet been forced on him.

Paul's Discourse as Grammar

A sense of God-forsakenness, abandonment, confusion, hopelessness, and helplessness lurks in the subtext of this letter. The danger of defection was real (4:3–8), and the need for encouragement was urgent. Paul's use of election language to address this issue reveals something of his pastoral heart.[8] Once Paul opens the letter, he immediately identifies the persecuted as the "beloved of God" whom God has chosen (*tēn eklogēn humōn,* 1:4). Then after reminding them of their reception of the gospel (1:5), Paul includes the persecuted in a partnership of suffering that includes, most notably, "the Lord" (1:6), the apostles whom they imitate, and the churches in Macedonia and Achaia for whom they are an example (1:7). If 2:14–16 is authentically Pauline and not a later editorial insertion, it expands the circle of suffering by noting, "You suffered the same things from your own compatriots as they did from the Jews" (2:14). This allusion to persecution is preceded by a paragraph recalling his own tender care for the Thessalonians and an admonition to "lead a life worthy of God, who calls you [*tou kalountos humas*] into his own kingdom and glory" (2:12). The immediate reference to persecution in 2:12–16 again appears to associate election and persecution. At times it appears that it is the destiny of the elect to suffer persecution for Christ. Paul wants no one to be "shaken by these persecutions. Indeed, [*gar*] you yourselves know that this is what we are destined [*keimetha*] for" (3:3; cf. 5:9). The word "destined" here stands a synonym of election. This huddling together against the cold is implicit also in Paul's language of participation, seen in phrases like "in Christ," "in God," and "in the Lord" (*en Christō, en theō,* and *en kuriō*; 1:1; 2:14; 4:16; 5:18; 4:1), in which he offers comfort to the dying by appealing to a presence that bridges the great divide. Paul's *en Christō* language is striking and unusual in 1 Thessalonians in the way it unites the living and dead in a common embrace. The emphasis on this "tie that binds" is obviously situational, for in the view of some, that tie had been irrevocably sundered by the unexpected and shocking death of some believers (4:16). Through his recitation of the final apocalyptic scenario, Paul thus joins the living elect with the departed saints in anticipation of Jesus' return.

First Thessalonians, however, is hardly one-dimensional, for Paul concerns himself not only with the destiny but also the ethos of the elect. What led Paul to tie election and holiness so intimately in 1 Thessalonians? Was this association designed to counter confusion, uncertainty, and ambiguity rising from persecution (Donfried), eschatological enthusiasm (Jewett), or the appeal of Hellenistic religion and philosophy (Malherbe)? Or are the community's sense of its destiny and its commitment to its ethos in the final analysis inseparable? If they are inseparable, the question remains as to why Paul felt compelled to discuss both here. Although we cannot know the answers to any of these questions with certainty, we can say that this association sharply separated the elect from the pagan world and helped secure the identity of the addressees against challenge and compromise.

In any case, in 4:7–8 Paul emphatically links the status of the elect with an ethos appropriate to that status. He begins by emphasizing holiness as a distinguishing mark of the elect: "For God did not call us to impurity [*akatharsia*] but in holiness [*hagiasmō*]. Therefore, whoever rejects this rejects not human authority but God, who also gives his Holy Spirit to you." In so attempting to define the elect rather than merely subverting the opposition,[9] Paul shares the outlook of the Holiness Code, in which Yahweh commands, "be holy, for I am holy" (Lev. 11:44, 45; 9:2; 20:26; etc.), but he makes no such association explicit. More than elsewhere Paul emphasizes the Holy Spirit (1:5, 6; 4:8), or spirit of the Holy One, as constitutive of the conduct of God's elect. This holiness sunders the holy from the unholy, from those acting immorally (*porneia*, 4:3), from "those not knowing God" (4:5), from the impure (4:7), from those "who have no hope" (4:13), from those who say "peace and security" during the eschatological crisis but know no peace (5:2), from those of the darkness (5:4), from children of the night (5:5), from the sleeping (5:6), and from the drunk (5:7). This separation defines the elect by giving them something to push against. Moreover, as in Jewish apocalyptic traditions, this separation not only *from* this pagan milieu but also *for* holiness is given an eschatological sanction: "Whoever rejects this rejects not human authority but God" (4:8). (Note a corresponding emphasis in 3:13 on holiness and blamelessness in light of the imminent coming [*parousia*] as the condition of the elect's existence.)[10] In spite of these echoes of Jewish apocalypticism and martyrological traditions, however, Paul nowhere in this letter seeks to associate either the divine election or the status and behavior of the elect with God's choice of the Jewish people. Had Paul thought through that connection, or is it absent simply because it was irrelevant in this discourse with a Gentile community? There is some evidence that both factors were at work. As we shall soon see, if we assume that 1 Thessalonians was Paul's earliest letter, there is evidence that Paul's view of election emerged as he faced new situations. That development, however, was evolutionary only from our perspective, for from Paul's angle of vision it was an attempt to understand the life of the elect in Christ in the revolution set in motion by the gospel of the end time. I recognize, however, that his emphasis on the communal aspects of election, holiness, and suffering may have suppressed conflicting voices and opinions. His stress on steadfastness in persecution may have masked both the nature of the resistance to his gospel and the degree of defection. And his unequivocal accentuation of cleanness, holiness, and morality may have concealed the level of ambivalence and doubt within the community about what one assigns to the world outside and what is tolerated inside. So even as we talk about development in Paul's theology we must be sensitive to the level of ambiguity and tension in this process that gives his theologizing a dynamic character.

PHILIPPIANS

Context of Paul's Grammar of Election

Even granting that no explicit reference to election appears in Philippians, traces of a grammar of election do occur both in Paul's language and in his address. As in 1 Thessalonians, Paul is less concerned here with the fact of election than with the status and marks of the elect. Whereas the epistolary context of the Thessalonians was suffused with uncertainty, hopelessness, and temptation to defect, inevitably associated with their persecutions, the letter to the Philippians reveals a partnership of suffering shared by the Philippian converts and Paul. The horrors of Paul's imprisonment and the threat of a possible, imminent execution, however, pervade the letter. Even as Paul writes, multiple exchanges take place between the beloved church in Philippi and the shackled apostle in mortal peril. The Philippians have sent Epaphroditus to minister to him, and perhaps from him Paul learned that Judaizers were undermining his gospel in Philippi. To Paul's worry about his own fate and rivals competing for the loyalty of the converts in Philippi is added his concern for Epaphroditus, who while ministering to the apostle has become critically ill. Meanwhile, the rivals back in Philippi have advocated circumcision as the initiation rite of admission to the elect community. Their libertinism has earned them the epithet "enemies of the cross of Christ" (3:18), and their appeal to their ancestral Jewish traditions has possibly encouraged the development of a spiritual hierarchy that Paul seeks to overturn. Even as Paul writes, he plans to dispatch Epaphroditus back to Philippi to offer a fuller report on the apostle and perhaps to bring a corrective and encouraging message from the apostle.

Paul's Language of Election

In this context Paul appeals to the language of his Jewish traditions, which had shaped his outlook, and uses language crafted by the experience of his confinement to define the status of the messianist elect. In addition to the mystical language of identification so common in 1 Thessalonians—the *en* language (*en Christō, en autō,* etc.)—this letter shares other parts of the Thessalonian language field. Even though the references to those in Christ (1:1; 3:1, 9, 14; 4:21) parallel those in 1 Thessalonians, the emphasis on "partnership [koinonia] in the gospel" is markedly stronger in Philippians (1:5, 7). Three additional metaphors appear in Philippians that are decidedly important. The first is an apocalyptic metaphor that Paul invokes to designate the holy elect as those who "shine as lights in the cosmos" (2:15), an apparent metaphor that refers to the *maskilim* as those who "shall shine like the brightness of the sky" taken either from Daniel (12:3) or *1 Enoch* (104:2). This association with the heavenly elect is implicit also in the second metaphor, which affirms the status of the elect "in Christ" as marginal inasmuch as they are resident aliens in this world, whose true colony (*politeuma*) is in heaven (3:20). The final metaphor springs from the polemical context of the letter as Paul draws on the most important rite of his native religion by addressing his church as the circumcision (*peritomē*). Notably, this small sample of language reveals a more direct appeal to the Jewish tradition than was the case in 1 Thessalonians, and the emphasis on the partnership of suffering, which was implicit in 1 Thessalonians, is more strongly emphasized here. Paul offers no reflection on the theological issue raised by his inclusion of Gentiles among the circumcision (not "true circumcision" as in the RSV), or among the heavenly luminaries. The solution to this theological conundrum is only latent and will later be developed by crisis.

Paul's Election Discourse as Grammar

The context noted above provoked Paul to draw explicitly on his own Jewish traditions and to introduce new language to interpret his own imprisonment and mortal peril and to define the status of his hearers, the messianist elect (cf. 4:21). In chapter 3 he calls up a vicious metaphor—"the dogs"—to describe those who are antithetical to the "circumcision," that is, the elect, who "worship in the Spirit of God and boast in Christ Jesus and have no confidence in the flesh" (3:2–3). Coopting the initiation rite of God's elect to refer to those in Christ, Paul twists the metaphor "circumcision" into an ugly pun to condemn his rivals as "those who mutilate the flesh." Although one might expect this metaphorical leap to cause him to reflect on the place of circumcision as a sign of God's covenant with Israel, it does not do so. Instead, he focuses on the proper ground of confidence by autobiographically recalling his Jewish legacy—circumcised, an Israelite, a Benjaminite, a super Hebrew, a Pharisee blameless under the law (3:5–6)—to deconstruct the religious claims of "those who mutilate the flesh." But just when Paul appears to have been a victim of his own silliness, substituting his own status claims for theirs, he appears to realize what he has done. Instantaneously he draws back, discarding them as "dung" (*skubala,* 3:8) in order that he may be found "in him," that is, in Christ (3:9). This spontaneous, visceral response to a serious challenge radically revalued the claims of the Judaizers and redefined "the circumcision" as those "in Christ." Paul was apparently unaware of the implications of his spiritualization of the sacral rite marking the elect or the bone of contention it would become in his relationship with the synagogue. It is stunning that this radical revaluation of circumcision did not lead to a repudiation of the physical circumcision of male initiates into the covenant community. If Paul failed to anticipate the angry explosion that his redefinition of circumcision would later ignite, he may be excused for lack of foresight, for the rules of the game in this setting had been set by the opposition, with their appeal to circumcision as a definitive mark of the elect. In the absence of the Galatian challenge his thinking was incomplete, and consequently his more limited response aimed to reinterpret the rules made and followed by his rivals in Philippi.

Paul's own imprisonment dominates the circumstances of Philippians. Even while fearing his execution was imminent (1:20–26), Paul seeks to honor Christ in his body "whether by life or by death" (1:20). In 2:17 he speaks metaphorically of his death as a sacrifice "as a libation over the sacrifice and the offering of your faith." Through sharing in Christ's sufferings, Paul hopes to become "like him in his death, if somehow I may attain the resurrection from the dead" (3:10–11), and he interprets this trajectory of suffering, death, and resurrection as the "upward call of God in Christ Jesus" (3:14). Giving these grim prospects a parenetic twist, Paul lifts them up as a model worthy of imitation by his addressees (3:17).[11] Thus, his imprisonment has become an occasion to urge the Philippians to "suffer for his [Christ's] sake, engaged in the same conflict [agōna] which you saw and now hear to be mine" (1:29–30 RSV). By appealing to his own suffering as a model and recalling the tradition of Christ's humiliation and death on a cross (2:5–11) Paul seeks to subvert the teaching of the "enemies of the cross of Christ" (3:17–18) and to offer a response to suffering very reminiscent of the martyrological traditions of Jewish apocalypticism. As an antidote to the fear, God-forsakenness, alienation, and anger that persecution brought, Paul substitutes a triumphant model and a partnership of suffering.[12]

Although Paul here relies on the language and cult of Judaism strikingly more than in 1 Thessalonians, he had not yet thought through the implications of his use of those traditions in light of the apocalyptic message he preached. Even though he called those in Christ "the circumcision" and the Judaizers "those who mutilate the flesh," he discounted the worth of his own circumcision and achievement as a Pharisee. Paul could call his own circumcision "dung" and the elect "the circumcision" in a wholly positive sense only because the metaphor of circumcision expanded the reach of the traditional rite in quite unexpected ways. He had yet to realize the implications of his metaphorical construction for assessing the traditions of Yahweh's covenant with Israel. He also had yet to understand the seriousness of the threat posed by the rival Jewish Christian missionaries. He was content here to excoriate the rivals without systematically contesting their teaching. As we shall see, that was soon to change.

GALATIANS

Context of Paul's Grammar of Election

Initially enthusiastic recipients of Paul's gospel, the Galatian church Paul had founded from a sickbed later cooled to the apostle and his message. After Paul's departure, the Galatian converts, either with external prompting or through internal disaffection, grew suspicious of the apostle and skeptical of the truth of his kerygma. Between the lines of the letter and mirrored in Paul's countercharges we see the attacks of his critics. Apparently some had pointed to Paul's derivative status, that is, his deference and subjection to the authority of the Jerusalem apostles, who claimed direct contact with the earthly Jesus. In the absence of any explicit instruction from Paul, the critics' emphasis on circumcision as the mark of election for Gentile male converts may have inclined the Galatians to take the command in Genesis 17:10 ("Every male among you shall be circumcised") with utmost seriousness. The warning that any uncircumcised male was to be "cut off" from God's people (Gen. 17:14) left little room for negotiation, and the threat, when linked with the practice of circumcision in Jerusalem by Jewish Christians, might have offered a warrant so compelling that the Galatian church felt obligated also to practice circumcision. If some such logic informed the Galatian practice and disagreement with Paul, we can better understand how the dispute between Paul and his converts was about the terms and marks of election rather than about the meaning of election itself.

In his response Paul expressed alarm over the Galatian understanding of the conditions of election. Rather than merely warning the Galatians about the circumcisers, Paul used some of his hottest rhetoric to contest their gospel.[13] The difference between the situations in Galatia and Philippi was dramatic. In Philippi, Paul enjoyed a warm and supportive partnership that existed from the beginning and continued with congregational support while he was in prison. Though Judaizers challenged his gospel in Philippi, he seemed unaware of the seriousness of the challenge of the Judaizing evangelists to his policy of including Gentiles without law observance as a prerequisite for membership in the people of God. Therefore, Paul merely warned the Philippians about the "dogs" without attempting to refute them. In Galatia, on the other hand, the far-reaching implications of that challenge were clear to Paul. The opposition found support in Scripture for its position and found in the example of the Jerusalem circle support for its views. The erosion of the Galatian church's support for Paul's gospel triggered a savage response. In his fiery defense, Paul's thinking about the distinguishing marks of election developed in some intriguing ways.

Paul's Language of Election

Galatians contains a rich collection of language that had previously shaped Paul's thinking and now is bent back onto the Galatian landscape in some ingenious ways. Space limits our discussion to three different though related language clusters dealing with the family, adoption, and calling. Interestingly, Paul's vocabulary about the family opens the letter, then disappears from the most polemical opening section of the body of the letter. For example, Paul addresses God as father (*pater*) three times in the salutation (1:1, 3, 4) and does not use the metaphor again until 4:2, 6. Those who claim God as father are here for the first time recognized by Paul as children of God (*huioi theou,* 3:26; 4:6, 7), though he did call the elect "children of light" in 1 Thessalonians 5:51. Here also for the first time Paul refers to the messianist believers as children of Abraham. Then Paul turns the Abraham narrative to his advantage to emphasize the familial status of Gentile believers as heirs (chaps. 3 and 4). Although Paul uses the term *eleutheria* in other ways elsewhere (e.g., 1 Cor. 4:14, 17; 7:14; 2 Cor. 6:13), here for the first time he addresses his readers as children of promise and children of freedom (4:31). And with the copious use of the metaphor *adelphoi,* or brothers and sisters, he privileges the relationship of the Galatian believers with God (Gal. 1:2, 11, 19; 3:15; 4:12, 28, 31; 5:11, 13; 6:1, 18). Although this rich vocabulary had shaped Paul's identity from childhood, he uses this vernacular in some highly creative ways. Nevertheless, his usage everywhere presumes a Jewish legacy. Intimately related to this metaphorical language field was Paul's discussion of adoption. Finally, his grammar of God's calling builds on the theology of election that we have noted in earlier letters. It is to Paul's treatment of calling, family, and adoption that we now turn.

Paul's Discourse on the Grammar of Election/Calling

Four explicit references to calling appear in Galatians aimed at refuting the gospel of the Judaizers (1:6, 15; 5:7–8, 13). The reference in 1:15 is only indirectly relevant since it deals not with God's election of Galatian believers but with the divine appointment of Paul as an apostle before his birth. By appealing to the experience of Jeremiah and Isaiah, whom God also chose before birth, Paul hoped to gain additional authority for his apostleship in his struggle against his Judaizing challengers, who obviously held quite a different theology of election. The first reference (1:6), however, enjoys pride of place. Expressing his astonishment that the Galatians were so quickly "deserting the one who called you in the grace of Christ," Paul articulates what was to be the central theme of the letter, namely, that God included Gentiles in the elect community by grace rather than by law observance.

In the reference in 5:7–8, Paul mixes praise and blame to win the loyalty of his converts. He praises the Galatians for having run so well, but scolds them for so quickly deserting the gospel. He asks, "Who prevented you from obeying the truth?" Then Paul categorically booms out, "Such persuasion does not come from the one who calls you." In other words, it is a human and even a perverse invention separating its adherents from the company of the elect and the realm of grace. This unambiguous rejection of the truth claims of his rivals aptly summarizes a theme that informs the entire letter: In 3:4 he accuses, "Did you experience so much for nothing?" In 4:11 he expresses the fear that his labor has been in vain and that they have fallen from grace. In 5:4 he reverses the warning of Genesis 17:9–14, which his opponents evidently claimed as foundational. There God commands Abraham to circumcise "every male among you" as a sign of the covenant, and warns, "Any uncircumcised male who is not circumcised in the flesh of his foreskin shall be cut off from his people; he has broken my covenant" (17:14). Radically reversing this warning, Paul holds instead that Gentile believers who accept circumcision post facto "want to be justified by the law" and "have cut [themselves] off from Christ" (5:4). In 5:6 he offers the premise of his critique of his rivals' preaching: "For in Christ Jesus neither circumcision nor uncircumcision counts for anything." To this Paul then pits his reconstructed antithesis: "The only thing that counts is faith working through love." At the end of the letter, Paul in his own hand repeats his devaluation of the primal rite that had always served as a sign of God's covenant people: "For neither circumcision nor uncircumcision is anything; but a new creation is everything!" (6:15). Paul aims not to establish Gentile Christianity as a new religion[14] but to undermine the practice of his adversaries, who sought to supplement his gospel to the Gentiles—which he judged to be sufficient in and of itself.

By taking love as the essence of election, Paul's final reference to calling (5:13) offers a positive balance to his earlier slashing attack on those who misunderstood both the nature and the ethos of election/calling: "For you were called [eklēthēte] to freedom, brothers and sisters; only do not use your freedom as an opportunity for self-indulgence, but through love become slaves to one another. For the whole law is summed up in a single commandment: 'You shall love your neighbor as yourself.'"[15] Instead of his earlier worry about the Galatians' deserting their calling, or his concern with their ignorance of the true precondition of election, Paul now paradoxically links freedom with communal obligation. Earlier he had denounced those devoted to the law; now he admonishes his converts to strictly observe the love commandment (Lev. 19:18, Gal. 5:14), and he does so without any evident sense that he is contradicting himself. How is one to understand this substitution of a prescription of law observance for his earlier rejection of law observance? Perhaps the answer lies in the role freedom played in the dispute. Paul's reminder of the call to freedom recalls and emphasizes the statement in 5:1: "For freedom Christ has set us free." Up to 5:13, "freedom" had been the flashpoint of conflict between Paul and his adversaries. In 5:13, however, Paul appears to anticipate charges that his law-free gospel was antinomian and encouraged immorality.[16] But here as elsewhere, Paul associates calling and moral behavior in an entirely traditional way. What is new here is the use of calling as a warning against defection and as a legitimate and necessary concomitant of the freedom he continues to proclaim in Christ. At stake in this discussion is what is the appropriate mark and ethos of the elect.

Paul's Discourse on the Grammar of Election/Adoption

The rivals' requirement of circumcision as a condition of and a distinguishing mark of the elect provoked Paul's angry response in a display of inspired exegesis. As noted earlier, the extent of the exploitation of family metaphors in Galatians has no precedent in earlier Pauline letters. The repeated emphasis on the recipients' status as children, or sons and daughters, in the letter to the Galatians is well known. The metaphor of father (*pater*) logically requires sons and daughters (*huioi*) or children (*tekna*). Perhaps in response to the scriptural exegesis of his antagonists, Paul now for the first time in his letters thinks exegetically about how Gentiles can be incorporated into God's family, Israel. Recalling Genesis 15–17, Paul offers a novel description in Galatians 3:15–19 of the election of the Gentiles. Through the faith of Christ, whom Paul calls Abraham's "offspring" (sing.), God found a way to include Gentiles as Abraham's offspring by adoption (*huiothēsian*, 4:5). These *adopted* children then become "heirs" (*klēronomoi*), a term Paul first uses here (Gal. 3:29; 4:1, 7). As his argument unfolds, Paul's thinking on this complex issue develops. How such adoption takes place Paul only gradually realized. As he groped his way through this complicated maze, the idea of the cross assumed a surprising nuance.

In 3:10 Paul's interpretation of Deuteronomy 27:26 (LXX) begins with a curse pronounced on all "who rely on the works of the law." Then follows in 3:13 a loose citation of Deuteronomy 21:23 which, Paul thought, pointed to Christ becoming a "curse"[17] through his crucifixion ("hanging on a tree"). The result of this "sin offering" was that "Christ redeemed us [Gentiles?] from the curse of the law by becoming a curse for us." How this happens Paul never tells us, but his hermeneutic gives the cross a unique inclusive sense: "in order that in Christ Jesus the blessing of Abraham might come to the Gentiles [*ta ethnē*]" (3:14). Here Paul expands the symbolism of the cross to argue for the legitimacy of the inclusion of the uncircumcised among the elect. Those included are none other than sons and daughters of God (3:26). These adopted children (4:5) may now address God with the familiar "Abba," and are no less heirs than the natural born (4:7).

The main point of Paul's allegorization of the Sarah and Hagar story (4:21–5:1) is the insertion of those formerly excluded into the inner circle as "children of the promise" and "children, not of the slave but of the free woman" (4:28, 31). Paul has not yet thought through the implications of excluding those belonging to the "present Jerusalem" (4:25), nor has he anticipated the profound theological questions that would be raised by his inclusion of Gentiles within "the Israel of God" (6:16).[18] These passages, however, are best read in light of the dispute in Galatia and Paul's feverish efforts to discredit the Judaizers and thereby to make the case for numbering uncircumcised Gentiles among the elect.

In these references we see how Paul's grammar of election was influenced by the traditions held in common with his adversaries. The battle, however, was over the proper reading of these texts. His adversaries read them in light of Jewish rites and religious practices sanctioned by centuries of use; Paul read them in light of the "new creation."[19] Nevertheless, the theological implications of Paul's hermeneutic vis-à-vis his ancestral religion were undeveloped. His interpretations of the Christ traditions were also in a formative stage, as shown by the way his response to various contexts shaped his view of the cross. For example, his use in this letter of the passion of Christ as a symbol for the inclusion of Gentiles among the elect goes far beyond its mimetic character in 1 Thessalonians and Philippians.

Paul's use of the cross to favor the inclusion of Gentiles qua Gentiles in the elect is ingenious and unique. This unparalleled usage shows how an attempt to find what is foundational in Paul's theology is risky. If the cross is at the core of Paul's theology, it is misleading to insist that the cross is foundational without noting the way the context affects Paul's interpretation and how that culturally conditioned interpretation is refracted through Paul back onto the context to shape that as well. This interactive relationship of symbol and setting is fundamentally unstable and resists efforts to find a core in Paul's theology that has a "totalizing" impact.[20] Even when allowing for Paul's creative or even inspired hermeneutic in defense of his Gentile gospel, in the eyes of his critics he went too far when he threatened Gentile male believers with being cut off from Christ if they accepted circumcision. Paul's threat suggested to some that God's promises to historic Israel could not be trusted. Such an assertion would raise fundamental questions about God's reliability. Those accusations soon elicited Paul's passionate defense of God's trustworthiness, which I shall discuss in the section on Romans.

1 CORINTHIANS

Context of Paul's Grammar of Election

Although persecution was a brutal fact for the Thessalonians, Philippians, and Galatians, no such grisly prospect frightened the Corinthians. No disillusionment clouded the outlook of the community, and no Judaizing rivals sought to discredit Paul's gospel. Instead, an eschatological enthusiasm prevailed, and the adventures in libertinism, boasting, spiritual elitism, claims to possess wisdom, and pretensions to holiness all threatened to fracture the community.[21] Their religious enthusiasm virtually eclipsed an emphasis on the cross (1:12–17). In place of an identification with the suffering and dying Christ, many found a mystical identification with the glorified Lord through surrogate mystagogues (1:12). They may have claimed the status of angels through their celibate marriages (7:1–5; Luke 20:34–36) and their ability to speak the language of angels through glossolalia (13:1). Paul's scornful description of them as full, rich, ruling, wise, strong, and honored (4:9–10) was obviously in their view a vicious caricature. But what they experienced as a dramatic and exciting spirit possession, Paul saw as destructive individualism, religious puffery (4:6, 18, 19; 5:2; 8:1; 13:4), and extremely waspish behavior that threatened to fragment the church.

Paul's Language of Election

Paul crafted his discussion of election, calling, and holiness to address this fractious behavior. The apostle's grammar of holiness includes temple allusions, references to unleavened bread, warning against participation in the rituals of idol worship, and allusion to a company of "holy ones," to which his hearers belonged. Paul includes a cluster of family metaphors (thirty-four references to the *adelphoi,* or brothers and sisters) that he may have used to correct centrifugal forces threatening the community. His sparing but important use of "father" in this letter (1:3; 8:6; 15:24) is also noteworthy. Most importantly, in this letter, Paul offers an interpretation of election/calling that is unparalleled.

Paul's Discourse as Grammar

In the salutation and thanksgiving of the letter, the apostle telegraphs his emphasis on the election theme, which threads its way through the letter. Paul's own call by God (1:1) is followed immediately by a reference "to the church of God that is in Corinth, to those who are sanctified in Christ Jesus, *called* [by God] to be saints" (1:2). Paul then concludes the thanksgiving by affirming the faithfulness of God through whom "you were *called* into the fellowship [*koinonian*] of his Son, Jesus Christ our Lord" (1:9). The conclusion of the thanksgiving is preceded by an expression of Paul's hope that his addressees will be established as "blameless on the day of our Lord Jesus Christ" (1:8). We see, therefore, that in both the salutation and the thanksgiving Paul links holiness and election, dual concerns that are complementary, though not always explicitly linked.

Holiness. In 1:18–2:5 Paul relativized the Corinthians' claims to wisdom, and in 3:5–17 he punctured their religious puffery with a barrage of metaphors— planting, irrigation, growing, building, and house burning. With this cluster of metaphors, Paul warned his readers facing the imminent judgment by fire to exercise their calling (election) with diligent care. The organizing metaphor of his kaleidoscope of images is the temple. The temple historically viewed as the epicenter of holiness, as the locus and authority for the sacral drama, as the organizing locus of Hebrew cosmology that stratified the social order, offered access to the divine presence and mediated atonement through the sacrificial cult. Whatever this symbol lacked for the Corinthians, it throbbed with life for Paul. After conjuring the temple metaphor, Paul links it to the church, and invokes God's curse on its desecrators: "Do you not know that you are God's temple and that God's spirit dwells in you [as the holy of holies]? If anyone destroys God's temple, God will destroy that person. For God's temple is holy, [and] you are that temple" (3:16–17). This symbolic rhetoric undermines individualistic holiness and affirms the mission of the holy ones by redirecting it to communal ends.

A similar strategy appears in 5:6–8. Paul uses the bread metaphor to warn a community in danger of fateful pollution to become what it is, that is, those "called to be saints" (1:2): "Cleanse out the old yeast so that you may be a new batch, as you really are unleavened" (5:7). In 6:1–11 he mocks the "saints" for acting like the immoral ones. In 6:12–20 he reminds those living by the slogan "All things are lawful" (6:12) that the spirit dwelling in their bodily temple is holy. Finally, in 10:14 he invokes a pagan temple metaphor to warn reckless adventurers to flee idolatry, because they "cannot drink the cup of the Lord and the cup of demons" (10:21). These creative expansions of metaphor appeal to rites, warnings, and admonitions to revise the Corinthian version of the holy life, which Paul sees as a sorry confusion of human urges mingled with piety.

Election. Inasmuch as Paul's addressees are called, Paul urges them to behave in a way befitting their status by separating themselves from pollution and to build up the "body." Only one paragraph after the thanksgiving, Paul challenges his converts to evaluate their claim to wisdom in light of their calling. Instead of appealing to the passion of Christ as an example (1 Thessalonians), Paul uses his own preaching of Christ crucified (1:18–25) and the election/calling of the Corinthians to undermine the Corinthian wisdom theology: "We proclaim Christ crucified, a stumbling block to Jews and foolishness to Gentiles, but to those who are the called, both Jews and Greeks, Christ the power of God and the wisdom of God" (1:23–24). From this summary of what Christ crucified means to the called, Paul moves directly into an ironic juxtaposition of human and divine wisdom, of human and divine strength (1:26–28).

Paul first orders the Corinthians to consider their calling: "Not many of you were wise by human standards, not many were powerful, not many were of noble birth" (1:26). He then concludes with a report on divine action that reversed this social hierarchy: "God chose what is foolish in the world to shame the wise; and God chose what is weak in the world to shame the strong; God chose what is low and despised in the world, things that are not, to reduce to nothing things that are" (1:27–28).

Paul takes for granted the hierarchical structure of the world. Yet he notes that in the divine choice (election) of the dregs of that order, God subverted the order itself and by implication the Corinthian hierarchy of spiritual gifts as well. Election (or calling) in and of itself undermines the Corinthian wisdom claims (1:30). God's calling thus exposes the arbitrariness and emptiness of hierarchical categories and turns this hierarchy on its head. Paul thus notes the self-contradiction of the Corinthian substitution of a charismatic hierarchy for a social one. Ironically, the Corinthian reversal still depends on the world's hierarchy for its primary model.[22]

In 12:27–31, Paul again challenges this charismatic hierarchy by constructing his own. And, as in 1:26–31, Paul links his construction with election language. Using "God has appointed" instead of "God chose," Paul assembles his model: "God has appointed in the church first apostles, second prophets, third teachers, then deeds of power, then gifts of healing, forms of assistance, forms of leadership, various kinds of tongues" (12:28). After asking rhetorically, "Are all apostles?" Paul challenges his readers: "Strive for the greater gifts" (12:31, presumably referring to those near the top of the list). It appears that Paul planned to use his own model to smash that of the Corinthians.

But just when the last piece of his model is in place, he pulls back. In a flash he seems to realize that what he has done is a contradiction; he has invented a hierarchy to subvert a hierarchy. Then in one stroke he dashes his model to bits: "I will show you a still more excellent way. If I speak in the tongues of mortals and of angels, but do not have love, I am a noisy gong or a clanging cymbal. And if I have prophetic powers, and understand all mysteries and all knowledge, and if I have all faith, so as to remove mountains, but do not have love, I gain nothing" (12:31–13:2). Love radically relativizes all spiritual gifts and the hierarchies they generate. Love, the quintessential eschatological gift, makes a mash of the Corinthian charismatic hierarchy. Thus, Paul chose not merely to smash one hierarchical model with another, but to show how love brings to light the arbitrariness and self-contradiction of the Corinthian model and his own as well. If Paul did what I have suggested that he might have done, his conversation about election aimed to redirect the Corinthian claim to superiority, to remove their grounds for boasting, and to illumine how love creates a new order. Scott Bartchy makes much the same point in his work on 1 Corinthians 7:21.[23] There he shows how Paul's discussion of slavery, celibacy, and marriage is related to his understanding of calling. Nine times in eight verses Paul uses some variant of the word "calling." If John C. Hurd is correct that 7:1 is a Corinthian slogan—"It is well for a man not to touch a woman"—then by appealing to Paul's celibacy, some in the community made holiness and celibacy correlates.[24] Paul, however, seeks to correct that understanding of calling and holiness by arguing that God's call subverts all advantages of rank and position, including religious rank. Thus, slavery was no handicap, in one's relationship to God, and being free no advantage; being uncircumcised was no handicap, and being circumcised no advantage; marriage was no handicap, and celibacy no advantage; not speaking in tongues was no handicap, and speaking in tongues no advantage. They all, as Bartchy notes, were "radically relativized by God's call."[25] Paul here not only deconstructs an elitist Corinthian theology but reconstructs a theology of election that is both concerned for others and free from the tyranny of the social order (7:23). Paul secures the identity of the Corinthians in the call of God rather than in an order established by circumcision or uncircumcision, slavery or freedom, marriage or celibacy. Paul urges the Corinthians to live as God has called them (7:17). Paul's fuller explication of what this way of life meant was to come later; here he aims to overturn a strategy that linked identity to one's social or religious status. This was an interpretation of his gospel that was revolutionary. Paul's openness to this radical possibility was, I believe, intimately tied to his location on an eschatological margin where he believed God had set him on the boundary between intersecting and warring ages. Without a location on the margin and the supreme eschatological gift offered in this overlap, the revolutionary possibility that he points to here would have been unthinkable.

ROMANS

Context of Paul's Grammar of Election

Whereas in 1 Corinthians Paul had articulated the implications of election for communal life in Corinth, and in Galatians Paul had defended his inclusive vision of election, in Romans he defended a view of election that his critics charged brought God's trustworthiness into question. If God had now gone to the Gentiles after pledging undying loyalty to Israel, then had God now defaulted on those promises and renounced the oaths plighted and promises made to this beloved one? Unlike 1 Corinthians, where Paul scolded enthusiastic sectarians, or Galatians, where he anathematized rival teachers, or 2 Corinthians, where he excoriated competing apostles, or Philippians, where he ridiculed Judaizing evangelists as "dogs," in Romans he addresses other issues. He faces troublesome conflicts between the "weak" and the "strong." He responds to the charge of preaching an antinomian Gentile gospel. He solicits the prayers of the Roman Christians for the successful delivery of the symbolic offering to Jerusalem, and he seeks support for his upcoming visit to Rome and his planned mission to Spain. More importantly, however, word may have circulated about the rather extreme position he took in his letter to the Galatians. Those familiar with the Scriptures would have known of God's pledge of faithfulness to Israel and of Israel's special status as God's elect (e.g., Gen. 15:5–20; 17:6–7; 18:19; 22:17–18; Hos. 2:21–23). Jewish messianists would have been riled by Paul's statement in Galatians that those who observed the law were enslaving themselves (Gal. 4:9; 5:1), and all who customarily circumcised male infants might have been scandalized by Paul's ugly pun that if they cut off their foreskins, they would be "cut off" from Christ (Gal. 5:2–4). Why would God condemn believers for observing what Scripture required? And did not this expansive and facile inclusion of "degenerate" pagans in the elect make a joke of the principle of divine justice? How can one endorse a gospel that has God choose the rejected and reject the chosen? In Romans 9–11 Paul attempts to respond to this serious indictment and seeks to offer a view of election that includes Gentile sinners without making a mockery of the veracity of God's promises to Israel.

Paul's Discourse of Election

Chapters 9–11 are the climax of rather than the appendix to chapters 1–8, and here for the first time Paul focuses on the significance of God's election of the Gentiles. (For that reason I will limit my discussion of election in Romans to these chapters.) Here Paul struggles with the implications of and justification for his Gentile mission. The pathos of Paul's words practically makes the text tremble in our hands: "I have great sorrow and unceasing anguish in my heart" (9:2). Like Moses, who offered his life as a sacrifice for a wayward people (Exod. 32:30–32), Paul offers his own life for Israel: "I could wish that I myself were accursed and cut off from Christ for the sake of my own people" (9:3). In his recognition of Israel's special status, Paul notes that to them belonged the glory, covenants, the law, the worship, and the promise of the Messiah "according to the flesh" (9:4–5). Nevertheless, he grieved that most of his kin found no place for them in the Jesus story. Paul still believed that God's covenant with Israel privileged the Jewish people, and he gave special priority in Romans to the Jews in God's economy of salvation (Rom. 1:16; 2:9, 10; 3:9, 29; 9:24). Now he offers a rationale for the inclusion of the "Gentile sinner" among God's elect. However, the question begging for a satisfactory answer was: Did this gospel speaking of God's turn to the Gentiles abrogate the historic promises to Israel? And if so, what kind of God was this who would pledge a covenant only to retract it? Had the word God historically plighted to Israel now failed?

Paul obviously recognized the indictment implicit in these questions, and it moved him to a vigorous response. He noted God is free to choose whomever. In an echo of the ancestral narrative that has Isaac privilege Jacob over the elder Esau, just as Abraham, at Sarah's prompting, had chosen Isaac over the elder half-brother, Ishmael, Paul defends God's freedom to privilege the younger, and asserts somewhat unconvincingly that such privileging is not unfair. Paul extends this scriptural precedent to account for God's choice of the Gentiles. Paul concludes then that God's choice is neither unfair (9:14–29) nor arbitrary, for all who turn to God will find salvation (9:30–10:21).

His denials notwithstanding, Paul's argument for divine freedom hardly answers the sharp indictment of his gospel. I have argued elsewhere that the major breakthrough comes less through assertion than through his introduction and development of the racing metaphor in 9:30–33. The scene Paul sketches there is almost farcical: Gentiles, collectively, who were hardly in the race, gained the righteousness prize. (Note that *diōkonta* in 9:30 means "run after" or "strain for.") Israel, however, who *was* running the race, tripped over a rock that God placed on the track! Israel tripped because it was running by works instead of faith, and failed to see Christ as the goal of its Torah or sacred story. But how could God fault Israel for not winning the prize when a divine agent placed a rock in the path of the runner? After the metaphor is introduced, it lies for a time undeveloped. Then as Paul ponders the division between those who gained the prize and those who failed (11:7–10), he recalls once more the image of Israel on the track and blurts out, "Have they stumbled so as to fall?" (11:11). Then he exclaims, "No, no! Absolutely not! But through stubbing their toes salvation has come to the Gentiles in order to make them [i.e., the Israelites] jealous" (my translation). This then will lead to the salvation of Israel, for "all Israel will be saved" (11:26). Paul then adds, "As regards the gospel they are enemies of God for your [i.e., Gentiles'] sake; but as regards election they are beloved, for the sake of their ancestors; *for the gifts and the calling of God are irrevocable*" (11:28–29). Up to now Paul had privileged Israel ahead of the Gentiles, but now a new strategy surprisingly emerges in which the old chronological order is reversed. In God's economy of salvation, enunciated by Paul, the Gentile is first, then the Israelite, but both are included![26]

The racing metaphor might have been suggested to Paul by the Isthmian games held every other year near Corinth, or by the legendary Olympic competition staged quadrennially since 776 B.C.E. Paul's Gentile converts in Corinth and his Roman readers would have known the popular story of the games staged to honor Patroclus, a fallen hero of the Trojan War. The story recalls how the goddess Athena intervened to fix the outcome of a foot race. In response to the prayer of the older, wily Odysseus running behind Aias, the swift and talented runner, Athena tripped Aias, sending him sprawling into the blood and gore of the sacrifices offered at the beginning of the race and allowing Odysseus to sprint to the finish line to win the race. Aias suffered ridicule and shame when he protested divine interference that gave the prize to Odysseus (Homer, *Iliad* 23.740–84). In the fiercely competitive games of the Hellenistic and Roman worlds, winners required losers, and the gods often intervened to guarantee the triumph of their favorites. The arduous training for sporting events took years, and on the winner was heaped laurels, lifelong honor and praise, while on losers was hung shame and disgrace. In Paul's invocation of the racing metaphor, he set up his reflection on the salvation race. Now he develops his earlier remark that Israel stumbled on a rock placed on the track by God. In Paul's world as in ours, winning was everything, and winners required losers. Now, almost in a flash, Paul has an insight that takes the breath away—a salvation race in which both the Israelites and the Gentiles would be winners. Paul himself seems almost overwhelmed by the idea. How can this be? It simply defies human reason, instinct, and custom. It is, Paul suggests, a great "mystery." The answer to the question is hidden in the mystery of the godhead itself. As Paul ponders this great "mystery," he can only wonder at it, and he launches into a soaring doxology: "O the depth of the riches and wisdom and knowledge of God! How unsearchable are his judgments and how inscrutable his ways! . . . For from him and through him and to him are all things. To him be the glory forever. Amen" (11:33–36).

Critics have questioned Paul's vision. Helmut Koester sees this daring initiative by Paul that included both Jew and Gentile as an effort "to accomplish the impossible."[27] Yet Paul might have given a different answer. Placed on the margin of the intersecting ages, that eschatological moment became for Paul an occasion for the articulation of a radical possibility, in which even the impossible is possible.

At the human level, however, Koester's observation is correct. Historically speaking, what Paul dreamed for, hoped for, and worked for came to an unfortunate end. Although Paul never lived to see the end of the story he inhabited, he had some intimations of the perils associated with his Gentile mission. As he had already suggested with his horticultural metaphor in 11:17–24, ingrafting wild olive shoots (Gentiles) into the domesticated stock (Israel) could lead to arrogance. Moreover, with the success of the Gentile mission there was the risk of developing a separated, sectarian, Gentile church, cut off from Israel. Considering the struggles he had to gain acceptance for his Gentile mission, he hardly foresaw the successful surge after his death that would eclipse the Jewish Christian dominance of his own day. Aflame with eschatological expectation whose genesis and fulfillment he located in Christ, Paul was able to live with ambiguity on the margin. And even though Paul endorsed the radical baptismal formula of Galatians 3:26 that erased in Christ any distinction between Jew and Greek, nevertheless, he could hardly envision an elect people of God without the theological entity of Israel. As Terence Donaldson well puts it, while "the boundary of Israel may have been radically redefined by Christ, nothing would alter the fact that Paul was ethnically as Jewish as his converts were (for the most part) Gentile."[28] The ambiguous "both/and" would soon be replaced by an "either/or," for the emerging church whose apocalyptic ardor had cooled was simply unable to live with the ambiguity that was a sine qua non of life on the margin.[29]

When Acts appeared a generation later, the expansion of the mission to the Gentiles seemed destined to prevail. By the time the deutero-Pauline Ephesians was written, the Jewish Christian community was in the minority and was at risk of being marginalized by a powerful Gentile majority.[30] The ugly exchanges between the Jewish Christian minority and Gentile Christian majority became especially shrill in the second century. Only too soon would the minority Jewish Christian church be tagged with the epithet "heretical." And Justin Martyr was not the last to describe the Gentile church as the "true Israel." The dream Paul had of an inclusive *ekklēsia* soured. In the end, Paul became something of a tragic figure.[31] He had suffered so much in his marginalized status to advance the radical vision of an inclusive church constructed on the margin. He had been beaten with rods, whipped with lashes, imprisoned, shipwrecked, maligned, and eventually, if tradition has it right, executed for his vision of an inclusive eschatological elect that made his Gentile converts adopted children of Abraham. Had he lived to see the failure of his vision, he would have been more than disappointed; he would have been heartbroken. Yet, given Paul's fertile mind, it would have been his contemporaries and not the God in Christ who would have blighted but not defeated his hope.

CONCLUSION

We have seen that Paul did not come to his context culturally naked. His grammar of election emerged in part from the language of the church about God, sin, Jesus Christ, the Spirit, righteousness, and the death, resurrection, and return of Jesus. His grammar was also informed by the venerable traditions and scriptures of Israel. The work of Paul the theologizer, however, can hardly be described by isolating these constituent elements as foundational. These elements are no bedrock for Paul, if by bedrock we mean a stable, static, unchangeable foundational element. We have seen how the language of Israel and of the Hellenistic church shaped the theological understanding of Paul, and how that in turn was further shaped by the context of the churches' requiring a response from Paul. Paul did not begin with a developed theology that merely shifted its emphasis from place to place. To be sure, his emphases and tactics did change, but in the letters we can actually see the process of theological formation taking place. We have noticed how Paul portrays the elect as those called to suffer with Christ (1 Thessalonians), as a community of believing Jews and Gentiles (Galatians), and as those chosen by God without regard for rank, position, or circumstance

(1 Corinthians). We have observed also that concern with the grammar of election involves not only observing Paul in the act of doing theology but also attending to the language field or larger field of discourse of election. We have seen how the cross, or Jesus' passion, which belongs to Paul's election grammar, may serve as a model for the persecuted (1 Thessalonians and Philippians), a symbol of inclusion (Galatians), and as a wrecking bar to dismantle hierarchical models of spiritual elitists (1 Corinthians). Election, thus conceived, is viewed less as a key propositional or foundational element than as an emerging, dynamic element in Paul's larger field of discourse.

I have argued throughout that Paul's life on the boundary of the ages accounts for the radical options he envisioned as a radical Jew. He was marginal, as bell hooks suggests, in a double sense. He was pushed to the margin by his critics in positions of power, and he was able to exploit that location as a scene of radical possibility. But his life on the margin possessed a dimension that bell hooks does not develop. He was absolutely convinced that God had assigned him, like Jeremiah, to his location on the margin. That margin was drawn to include the overlap between worlds in collision, and was infused with an apocalyptic dynamism and power. It was enlivened by Paul's sense that he stood on the cusp of history awaiting the completion of the dramatic, revolutionary advent of God's new order. In that electrically charged, exciting and dreadful atmosphere alive with possibility, Paul set out on his godly mission to the Gentiles. Although he was certain of his loyalty to Christ, his task and location were fraught with ambiguity. Paul's convictions and fertile mind combined to exploit that location to articulate a vision that was so daring and so demanding that it was soon compromised, and yet it remained in these seven occasional letters to subvert the very compromises made.

Notes

Preface

1. Calvin J. Roetzel, *Paul: The Man and the Myth* (Minneapolis: Fortress Press, 1999), 2.
2. Daniel Boyarin, "The IOUDAIOI in John and the Prehistory of 'Judaism,'" in *Pauline Conversations in Context: Essays in Honor of Calvin J. Roetzel,* ed. Janice Capel Anderson, Philip Sellew, and Claudia Setzer (Sheffield: Sheffield Academic Press, 2002), 216–39.

Chapter 1

1. Bell hooks, "Choosing the Margin as a Space of Radical Openness," in *yearning: race, gender, and cultural politics* (Boston: South End Press, 1990), 145–55, esp. 149.
2. Ibid., 153.
3. Ibid., 118.
4. John P. Meier, *A Marginal Jew: Rethinking the Historical Jesus* (New York: Doubleday, 1991), 9.
5. Ibid., 6–9.
6. Jürgen Becker, *Paul, Apostle to the Gentiles*, trans. O. C. Dean Jr. (Louisville, Ky.: Westminster/John Knox Press, 1993), 33.
7. Adolf von Harnack, "The Founder of Christian Civilization," in *The Writings of St. Paul*, ed. Wayne A. Meeks (New York: W. W. Norton & Co., 1966), 302.

89

8. On this point I differ with Terence L. Donaldson, *Paul and the Gentiles: Remapping the Apostle's Convictional World* (Minneapolis: Fortress Press, 1997), who argues that Paul substituted Christ for Torah.

9. Some readers here will recognize the influence of Victor Turner, *The Ritual Process: Structure and Anti-Structure* (Ithaca, N.Y.: Cornell University Press, 1969). The ambiguity of life in this liminal location, however, goes beyond ritual, as Turner himself recognized. See his "Myth and Symbol," in *The International Encyclopedia of Social Sciences*, ed. David L. Sills (New York: Macmillan and the Free Press, 1968), 10:576–79.

10. This represents another point of disagreement with Donaldson, who holds that at his "conversion" Paul's core convictions were set for the rest of his life.

11. Quoted in Edgar Hennecke, *New Testament Apocrypha*, rev. ed., ed. W. Schneemelcher, trans. R. McL. Wilson, 2 vols. (Philadelphia: Westminster Press, 1963), 122–23.

12. See J. Andrew Overman, "Kata Nomon Pharisaios: A Short History of Paul's Pharisaism," in *Pauline Conversations in Context: Essays in Honor of Calvin J. Roetzel*, ed. Janice Capel Anderson, Philip Sellew, and Claudia Setzer (Sheffield: Sheffield Academic Press, 2002), 180–93.

13. Paul does not categorically reject his Pharisaic past, but radically qualifies it in light of his experience of the Christ. In many ways, vestiges of that Pharisaism remain to inform his discourse.

14. See Calvin J. Roetzel, *Paul: The Man and the Myth* (Minneapolis: Fortress Press, 1999), 30–38.

15. Janice Perlman, *The Myth of Marginality: Urban Poverty and Politics in Rio de Janeiro* (Berkeley: University of California Press, 1976), 129.

16. Ibid., 242.

17. In her work cited, Perlman speaks poignantly of the struggle of migrants in a shantytown in Rio de Janeiro, who in spite of their marginalization integrated into the majority culture, worked very hard at the most onerous tasks in service sector jobs, maintained their long-term optimism, sacrificed to raise their families, and conducted their lives in the most adverse circumstances with a gentle dignity. Perlman thus argues that the myth of marginality is a fabrication of those in power to control and diminish this underclass.

18. Such a reading of life on the margin well comports with hooks's view of the margin as a location of radical possibility. See her "Choosing the Margin as a Space of Radical Openness," n. 1 above.

Chapter 2

1. A. D. Nock, *Conversion: The Old and New in Religion from Alexander the Great to Augustine of Hippo* (Oxford: Oxford University Press, 1933), 7; emphasis added.

2. Ibid., 10.

3. Jürgen Becker, *Paul, Apostle to the Gentiles,* trans. O. C. Dean Jr. (Louisville, Ky.: Westminster/John Knox Press, 1993), 62.

4. Ibid., 77; emphasis added.

5. Ibid.

6. Ibid., 33.

7. Marion Soards, introduction to Becker, *Paul,* 2.

8. Krister Stendahl, *Paul among Jews and Gentiles and Other Essays* (Philadelphia: Fortress Press, 1976), 9. See his chapter titled "Call Rather than Conversion," 7–23.

9. See Beverly Roberts Gaventa, *From Darkness to Light: Aspects of Conversion in the New Testament* (Philadelphia: Fortress Press, 1986); see esp. 151.

10. Gaventa, *From Darkness to Light,* 148.
11. Alan Segal, *Paul the Convert: The Apostolate and Apostasy of Saul the Pharisee* (New Haven, Conn.: Yale University Press, 1990), 72.
12. Ibid., 93.
13. See her award-winning book, *Jesus as Mother: Studies in the Spirituality of the High Middle Ages* (Berkeley and Los Angeles: University of California Press, 1982) and "'. . . And Woman His Humanity': Female Imagery in the Religious Writing of the Later Middle Ages," in *Gender and Religion: On the Complexity of Symbols,* ed. Caroline Walker Bynum, Stevan Harrell, and Paula Richman (Boston: Beacon Press, 1986).
14. "Introduction: The Complexity of Symbols," in *Gender and Religion: On the Complexity of Symbols,* 13.
15. "'. . . And Woman His Humanity': Female Imagery in the Religious Writing of the Later Middle Ages," in *Gender and Religion: On the Complexity of Symbols,* ed. Byrum *et al.,* 269.
16. Ibid., 268, 270.
17. Ibid., 265.
18. Ibid.
19. Ibid., 200.
20. Ibid., 13.
21. Ibid., 273.
22. Ibid.
23. Ibid., 274.
24. See Beverly R. Gaventa, "The Maternity of Paul: An Exegetical Study of Galatians 4:19," in *Conversation Continues: Studies in Paul and John in Honor of J. Louis Martyn,* ed. Robert T. Fortna and Beverly R. Gaventa (Nashville: Abingdon Press, 1990), 189–201; and "Apostles as Babes and Nurses in 1 Thessalonians 2:7," in *Faith and History: Essays in Honor of Paul W. Meyer,* ed. John T. Carroll, Charles H. Cosgrove, and E. Elizabeth Johnson (Atlanta: Scholars Press, 1990), 193–207.
25. See Steve Kraftchick, "Death in Us, Life in You: The Apostolic Medium," in *Pauline Theology,* vol. 2, *1 and 2 Corinthians,* ed. David M. Hay (Minneapolis: Fortress Press, 1993), 156–81.
26. Cited in Bynum, "'. . . And Woman His Humanity,'" 264.
27. Ibid.
28. This tendency here is consistent with what we see elsewhere in Paul's letters. In 1 Corinthians 16:22, he threatens those who do not love the Lord with a curse—that is, damnation; in 1 Corinthians 4:21, he threatens a recalcitrant and fractious church with punishment "with a rod"; in 1 Corinthians 5:3–5, he pronounces judgment on a wayward believer from afar, calling for his excommunication. This imagery is reversed in Philippians 1:1, where Paul assumes the role of a slave patterned after Christ, who "emptied himself, taking the form of a slave" (Phil. 2:7). In his letter to the Roman church, a church he had neither founded nor visited, a church that may have been suspicious of Paul and his gospel, his first words were "Paul, a slave of Christ Jesus . . ."
29. See Gaventa, "Apostles as Babes and Nurses," 194–98.
30. Gaventa, "Apostles as Babes and Nurses," 203–207.
31. Ibid., 204–207.
32. See the discussion of "Nutrix" in August Friedrich von Pauly, *Realencyclopädie der Classischen Altertumswissenschaft* (Stuttgart: Alfred Drückenmüller Verlag, 1937), 1493–1501.
33. A very old but still valuable discussion of the nurse in antiquity may be found in Mary Rosaria Gorman's "The Nurse in Greek Life" (unpublished Ph.D. diss., Catholic University, 1917).

34. See Johannes Munck, *Paul and the Salvation of Mankind*, trans. Frank Clarke (Richmond, Va.: John Knox Press, 1959), 11–35.
35. Adolf von Harnack, "The Founder of Christian Civilization," from *What Is Christianity?* trans. Thomas Bailey Saunders (New York: Harper, 1957), 190.

Chapter 3

1. See Quintin Hoare and Geoffrey Noel Smith, trans., *Selections from the Prison Notebooks of Antonio Gramsci* (London: Lawrence & Wishart; New York: International, 1971), 10; and Cornel West, *Prophesy Deliverance: An Afro-American Revolutionary Christianity* (Philadelphia: Westminster Press, 1982), chap. 1.
2. See John J. Collins, *The Apocalyptic Imagination: An Introduction to the Jewish Matrix of Christianity* (New York: Crossroad, 1984), 30, following Jonathan Z. Smith, "Wisdom and Apocalyptic," in *Syncretism in Antiquity: Essays in Conversation with Geo Widengren*, ed. Birger A. Pearson (Missoula, Mont.: Scholars Press, 1975), 131–56, repr. in *Visionaries and Their Apocalypses*, ed. Paul D. Hanson, Issues in Religion and Theology 4 (Philadelphia: Fortress Press; London: SCM Press, 1983), 115-40.
3. Ernst Käsemann, "The Beginnings of Christian Theology," in *New Testament Questions of Today* (Philadelphia: Fortress Press; London: SCM Press, 1969), 102 (German original in *ZTK* 57 [1960]: 162–85). See further his "On the Subject of Primitive Christian Apocalyptic," in *New Testament Questions*, 108–37, esp. 137. (Käsemann's German noun *Apokalyptik* is almost universally mistranslated in English as the adjective "apocalyptic" rather than the noun "apocalypticism.") Käsemann had been greatly influenced by Albert Schweitzer's work on apocalypticism, and in at least one sense they were kindred spirits. On the Ogowe steamer on St. Stephen's Day, 1929, Schweitzer began the preface to his *Mysticism of Paul the Apostle*, and before the steamer docked in Lambarene he had rounded off the introduction with a final flourish: "Just because Paul's mystical doctrine of Christ has more to say to us when it speaks to us in the fire of its primitive-Christian, eschatological, manner of thought than when it is paraphrased into the language of modern orthodoxy or modern unorthodoxy, I believe I am serving in this work the cause not only of sound learning but also of religious needs" (Albert Schweitzer, *The Mysticism of Paul the Apostle* [London: Black, 1931], x).
4. Rudolf Bultmann, "Ist die Apokalyptik die Mutter der christlichen Theologie? Eine Auseinandersetzung mit Ernst Käsemann," in *Apophoreta: Festschrift für Ernst Haenchen zu seinem siebzigsten Geburtstag am 10. Dezember, 1964*, Herausgeber, Walther, and Hester, BZNW 30 (Berlin: Töpelmann, 1964), 64–69.
5. Philip Vielhauer, "Apocalyptic in Early Christianity," in *New Testament Apocrypha*, vol. 2, ed. Edgar Hennecke and Wilhelm Schneemelcher (Philadelphia: Westminster Press, 1965), 609.
6. Hans Conzelmann, "On the Analysis of the Confessional Formula in 1 Corinthians 15:3–5," *Int* 20 (1966): 15-25. See especially note 16 with its polemic against Käsemann.
7. Willi Marxsen, *Introduction to the New Testament: An Approach to Its Problems* (Philadelphia: Fortress Press, 1968), 273.
8. E. P. Sanders, *Paul and Palestinian Judaism: A Comparison of Patterns of Religion* (Philadelphia: Fortress Press, 1977), 543.
9. Robin Scroggs, "Ernst Käsemann: The Divine Agent Provocateur," *RelSRev* 11 (1985): 261.
10. See Abraham J. Malherbe, *Social Aspects of Early Christianity* (Baton Rouge: Louisiana State University Press, 1977).

11. Johan Christiaan Beker, *Paul the Apostle: The Triumph of God in Life and Thought* (Philadelphia: Fortress Press, 1980), 16–17, 135.

12. Ibid., 207.

13. The nature of Paul's apocalypticism is debated. The dispute has been influenced by the Society of Biblical Literature Genres Project, on which Collins reports in his *Apocalyptic Imagination.* That study discredited many older, simplistic definitions of apocalypses and provided valuable help in describing the structure, context, and complexity of apocalypses. Collins in particular questions the value of essentialist definitions that describe apocalypses thematically (e.g., as dualistic, pseudepigraphic, forensic, or as dealing with reversal, angels, and the like). He prefers instead the definition hammered out by the members of the Genres Project, in which *apocalypse* is defined as "a genre of revelatory literature with a narrative framework, in which a revelation is mediated by an otherworldly being to a human recipient, disclosing a transcendent reality which is both temporal, insofar as it envisages eschatological salvation, and spatial, insofar as it involves another, supernatural world" (Collins, *Apocalyptic Imagination,* 4). Others, such as Sanders, have found this definition too general; see E. P. Sanders, "The Genre of Palestinian Jewish Apocalypses," in *Apocalypticism in the Mediterranean World and the Near East,* ed. David Hellholm (Tübingen: J. C. B. Mohr [Paul Siebeck], 1983), 447–59.

14. See Mary Douglas, *Purity and Danger: An Analysis of Concepts of Pollution and Taboo* (London: Routledge & Kegan Paul; New York: Praeger, 1966).

15. Wayne A. Meeks has drawn attention to this language of separation in *The First Urban Christians: The Social World of the Apostle Paul* (New Haven, Conn.: Yale University Press, 1983), 84–96.

16. Translation in Florentino Garcia Martinez, *The Dead Sea Scrolls Translated: The Qumran Texts in English,* 2d ed. (Leiden: E. J. Brill; Grand Rapids: Wm B. Eerdmans Publishing Co., 1996), 8.

17. Krister Stendahl holds otherwise. He has argued that Paul's motivation for non-retaliation parallels that of Qumran—i.e., that given the impending wrath, one can eschew retaliation knowing that God will soon vindicate that righteousness completely ("Hate, Non-retaliation, and Love: 1QS x.17–20 and Rom. 12:19–21," *HTR* 55 [1962]: 343–55; repr. in Krister Stendahl, *Meanings: The Bible as Document and as Guide* [Philadelphia: Fortress Press, 1984], 137–49). While the apocalyptic motivation does inform Paul's exhortation (see Rom. 13:11: "Salvation is nearer to us now than when we became believers"), the apocalyptic element reinforces and energizes love for the outsider, not vice versa. On other grounds but supporting the position here, see James D. G. Dunn, *Romans 9–16,* WBC 38B (Dallas: Word, 1988), 749–52, 755–56.

18. Stendahl, "Hate, Non-retaliation, and Love," 341.

19. Paul apparently shares this understanding with Matt. 24:12: "The love of many will grow cold."

20. See John G. Gager, *Kingdom and Community: The Social World of Early Christianity* (Englewood Cliffs, N.J.: Prentice-Hall, 1975).

21. Whether this was a spiritual marriage, as John Coolidge Hurd allows for *(The Origins of First Corinthians* [London: SPCK, 1965], 277–78), or not, as Gerhard Sellin holds ("Hauptprobleme des Ersten Korintherbriefes," *ANRW* 2.25.4 [1994], 2970–72) and as Gordon D. Fee asserts (*The First Epistle to the Corinthians* [Grand Rapids: Wm B. Eerdmans Publishing Co., 1987], 198–213), is not germane, although Sellin and Fee seem to make too little of the fact that the man is doing this "in the name of the Lord Jesus."

22. See Arnold van Gennep, *Rites of Passage* (Chicago: University of Chicago Press, 1960; French original, 1909).

23. See Victor Turner, *The Ritual Process: Structure and Anti-Structure* (London: Routledge & Kegan Paul; Ithaca, N.Y.: Cornell University Press, 1969); see also Turner, "Myth and Symbol," in *The International Encyclopedia of the Social Sciences,* ed. David L. Sills, 17 vols. in 8 (New York: Macmillan, 1972), 10:576–79.

24. Richard A. Horsley's description of the apocalyptic enthusiasm in Corinth as "spiritual elitism" is apt; see his "'How Can Some of You Say There Is No Resurrection of the Dead?' Spiritual Elitism in Corinth," *NovT* 20 (1978): 203–31.

25. Fee holds this view; see note 21.

26. Collins, *Apocalyptic Imagination,* 214.

27. As the late John Gammie once pointed out to me, Daniel looks forward to the reinstitution of sacrifice in Jerusalem; one might also mention the so-called Animal Apocalypse in *1 Enoch* 90:18–19, which endorses armed revolt against the oppressors of this world.

28. Rudolf Bultmann, *New Testament Theology,* 2 vols. (London: SCM Press; New York: Charles Scribner's Sons, 1951–1955), 1:256, viewed this passage as an anthropological description of the human condition prior to faith, but he failed to do justice to the strong apocalyptic connotation of the act of deliverance. J. Louis Martyn makes a compelling case for the apocalyptic intent of the letter in "Apocalyptic Antinomies in Paul's Letter to the Galatians," *NTS* 31 (1985): 410–24.

29. Here I am obviously at odds with Ronald F. Hock, *The Social Context of Paul's Ministry: Tentmaking and Apostleship* (Philadelphia: Fortress Press, 1988).

30. See, e.g., Günther Bornkamm, *Paul* (New York: Harper & Row, 1971), 213; and Ernst Käsemann, *Commentary on Romans* (Grand Rapids: Wm. B. Eerdmans Publishing Co., 1980), 361.

31. Turner, "Myth and Symbol," 577.

32. Turner, *Ritual Process,* 102.

33. See Hurd, *Origins of First Corinthians,* 157; similarly Robin Scroggs, "Paul and the Eschatological Woman," *JAAR* 40 (1972): 283–303; Wayne A. Meeks, "The Image of the Androgyne: Some Uses of a Symbol in Earliest Christianity," *HR* 13 (1974): 165–208; S. Scott Bartchy, *Mallon Chresai: First-Century Slavery and the Interpretation of 1 Corinthians 7:21,* SBLDS 11 (Missoula, Mont.: Scholars Press, 1973), 127–55.

34. Note Paul's significant omission of the phrase "male and female" in his recitation in 1 Cor. 12:13 of the baptismal formula quoted in full in Gal. 3:28.

35. See David Daube, "Pauline Contributions to a Pluralistic Culture: Re-Creation and Beyond," in *Jesus and Man's Hope,* ed. Donald G. Miller and Dikran Y. Hadidian (Pittsburgh: Pittsburgh Theological Seminary, 1971), 2:223–45.

36. Turner, *Ritual Process,* 103–10.

37. Birger A. Pearson's arguments against the authenticity of 1 Thess. 2:13–16 are to me compelling ("1 Thessalonians 2:13–16: A Deutero-Pauline Interpolation," *HTR* 64 [1971]: 79–94), but see now Robert Jewett, *The Thessalonian Correspondence: Pauline Rhetoric and Millenarian Piety,* FF (Philadelphia: Fortress Press, 1986), 36–42.

38. See Calvin J. Roetzel, *Judgment in the Community: A Study of the Relationship between Eschatology and Ecclesiology in Paul* (Leiden: E. J. Brill, 1972).

39. See the excellent treatment of this passage in John E. Toews, "The Law in Paul's Letter to the Romans: A Study of Rom. 9:30–10:13" (Ph.D. diss., Northwestern University, 1977).

40. See my review of Norman R. Peterson, *Rediscovering Paul: Philemon and the Sociology of Paul's Narrative World* (Philadelphia: Fortress Press, 1985) in *ThTo* 43 (1986): 139–42. There I argue that Paul's gospel may implicitly suggest that

Onesimus, the slave, be given his freedom, but this hardly means that Paul required Philemon to manumit him. A rich humanitarian tradition seems to obscure Peterson's understanding of Paul at this point. No resolution is apparent to this reader concerning Onesimus's ambiguous status as a Christian slave.

41. I am grateful to Jouette M. Bassler for reading an earlier version of this essay and offering many valuable suggestions for its improvement.

Chapter 4

1. The experience of Helen Keller proved the truth of Wittgenstein's philosophy of language. See *Wittgenstein: Lectures and Conversations on Aesthetics, Psychology, and Religious Belief*, ed. Cyril Barrett (Berkeley, Calif.: University of California Press, 1966), which also influenced George A. Lindbeck and Wayne Proudfoot.

2. Rudolf Bultmann, *Theology of the New Testament*, trans. Kendrick Grobel (New York: Charles Scribner's Sons, 1954), 1:63.

3. Walter Schmithals follows Bultmann in calling them Gnostics. Dieter Georgi argued that they were Hellenistic Jewish Christian missionaries who modeled their ministry after the "god man" (*theos anēr*), or miracle worker, of popular Hellenistic religion. Ernst Käsemann and C. K. Barrett hold them to be missionaries of the Palestinian church sent out as a truth squad to correct Paul's faulty gospel. Hans Dieter Betz, in turn, sees them as missionaries profoundly influenced by Cynic philosophy and Sophist propaganda.

    Each position has merit, but each also has weaknesses. Given the lack of evidence for a full-blown Gnosticism in the first century, Schmithal's position has been dismissed as anachronistic. David Tiede and Carl Holladay have questioned Georgi's *theos anēr* construction. Because of the absence of any debate about the law in 2 Corinthians, it is unlikely that Paul's critics came from the Jerusalem church, as Käsemann and Barrett hold, and Betz's attempt to root the opposition in Cynic and Sophist positions understates the Jewish provenance of Paul's opponents (2 Cor. 11:22–23). With reservations, however, I prefer Georgi's position, which allows for both the Jewish and Hellenistic character of Paul's opposition.

4. See Dieter Georgi, *The Opponents of Paul in Second Corinthians* (Philadelphia: Fortress Press, 1986).

5. George Lyons, *Pauline Autobiography: Toward a New Understanding* (Atlanta: Scholars Press, 1985), 107–12, reads the antithetical constructions in 1 Thessalonians and Galatians as rhetorical statements not designed to deny the first statement but to emphasize the second. In 2 Corinthians, however, the polemic is so near the surface that it is hard to believe that the antitheses do not have a polemical character.

6. See A. J. M. Wedderburn, *Baptism and Resurrection: Studies in Pauline Theology against Its Graeco-Roman Background* (Tübingen: J. C. B. Mohr [Paul Siebeck], 1987), 389, where he follows with qualification Herbert Braun, "Das 'Stirb und Werde' in der Antike und im Neuen Testament," in *Gesammelte Studien zum Neuen Testament und seiner Umwelt* (Tübingen: J. C. B. Mohr [Paul Siebeck], 1967), 136–58.

7. Note 2 Cor. 12, where Paul juxtaposes visions against hardship in the service of the gospel.

8. See James M. Robinson, "The Historicality of Biblical Language," in *The Old Testament and Christian Faith*, ed. Bernhard W. Anderson (New York: Harper & Row, 1963), 132–49.

9. It is unlikely that the rivals actually preached a gospel of self-sufficiency, but Paul drew the conclusion that they did from their behavior.

10. My debt here to Steven Kraftchick is obvious. See his "Death's Parsing: Experience as a Mode of Theology in Paul," in *Pauline Conversations in Context: Essays in Honor of Calvin J. Roetzel*, ed. Janice Capel Anderson, Philip Sellew, and Claudia Setzer (Sheffield: Sheffield Academic Press, 2002), 144–66.

11. Georgi has argued that from 2:16 on Paul is engaged in sharp polemic. Given the contrast here between Paul's experience and that of the rival apostles, it appears that Paul's polemic does, at least implicitly, begin here.

12. See Scott J. Hafemann, *Suffering and the Spirit: An Exegetical Study of II Cor. 2:14–3:3 within the Context of the Corinthian Correspondence* (Tübingen: J. C. B. Mohr [Paul Siebeck], 1986). See also P. Marshall, "A Metaphor of Social Shame: *Thriambeuein* in 2 Cor. 2:14," *NovT* 25 (1983): 302–17.

13. This quotation is from the paper, "Paul as Strong Poet: Metaphor, Irony, and Redescription in Pauline Theology," which Kraftchick delivered at the 1990 meeting of the Society of Biblical Literature.

14. Victor P. Furnish, *II Corinthians* (Garden City, N.Y.: Doubleday, 1984), 187.

15. Ibid., 278.

16. Their Stoic and Cynic background was first noted by Rudolf Bultmann, *Der Stil der paulinischen Predigt und die kynisch-stoische Diatribe* (Göttingen: Vandenhoeck & Ruprecht, 1910), 71–80. See also his *Der zweite Brief an die Korinther*, ed. E. Dinkler (Göttingen: Vandenhoeck & Ruprecht, 1976), 170–76. Although Bultmann saw a Stoic literary connection, the understanding of suffering that Paul offers is quite different. Through the acknowledgment of the way Logos suffused and governed the world, the Stoic sought to arrive at a state of *apatheia* ("apathy") in which one would be unaffected by life's peril or pain. Paul, however, was affected, and it was by God's power that he was encouraged in the present and hoped to be vindicated in the future.

17. Sylvia Plath, "All the Dead Dears," in *The Collected Poems,* ed. Ted Hughes (New York: Harper & Row, 1981), 70.

18. See W. L. Knox, *St. Paul and the Church of the Gentiles* (Cambridge: Cambridge University Press, 1939), who argues that Paul completely revised his eschatology between the writing of 1 Thessalonians, in which he expects to be alive at Jesus' parousia, and this letter, where he accepts the Greek understanding of the afterlife in which the soul is robed with a divine cloak of fire. My opening remarks, however, argue that Paul's view of the resurrection and the afterlife is traditionally Jewish and Christian.

19. See Bultmann, *Zweite Brief an die Korinther*, and Walter Schmithals, *Gnosticism in Corinth*, trans, J. E. Steely (Nashville: Abingdon Press, 1971).

20. Furnish, *II Corinthians*, 288.

21. See Friedrich Lang, *2 Korinther 5, 1–10 in der neueren Forschung* (Tübingen: J. C. B. Mohr [Paul Siebeck], 1973).

22. Ibid., 194.

23. Ralph Martin, *2 Corinthians* (Waco, Tex.: Word, 1986), 101.

Chapter 5

1. I am grateful to the Trial Balloon Society for its critique of this chapter, which first appeared in a volume honoring A. T. Kraabel, one of the charter members of the Trial Balloon Society, whose work on Diaspora Judaism has placed biblical scholarship in his debt.

2. See Nils Dahl, "The One God of Jews and Gentiles (Romans 3:29–30)," in his *Studies in Paul: Theology for the Early Christian Mission* (Minneapolis: Augsburg, 1977), 178–91.

3. This chapter was inspired by the work of David Tracy, *Plurality and Ambiguity* (San Francisco: Harper & Row, 1987), and the recent concerns of Martin E. Marty.

4. The LXX hardly received universal endorsement, despite the defense of its accuracy and authority by both Psuedo-Aristeas and Philo. Some shadow was cast on the LXX by Jesus ben Sirach (ca. 132 B.C.E.), for "what was originally expressed in Hebrew does not have exactly the same sense when translated into another language" (Emil Schürer, *The History of the Jewish People in the Age of Jesus Christ*, rev. and ed. Geza Vermes, Fergus Millar, and Martin Goodman [Edinburgh: T. & T. Clark, 1986], III, 477).

5. Works not serving as direct commentary on the LXX are *That Every Good Person Is Free, On the Contemplative Life, On the Eternity of the World, Against Flaccus, Hypothetica, On Providence,* and *On the Embassy to Gaius.* Volumes 1–7 of Philo's writings all serve as commentary on the Pentateuch of the LXX.

6. A substantial bibliography of secondary literature on the LXX is available. For a survey of the literature see E. Tob, "Die griechischen Bibelübersetzung," *ANRW* 20.1, 121–89, and his "Jewish Greek Scriptures," in *Early Judaism and Its Modern Interpreters*, ed. Robert A. Kraft and George W. E. Nickelsburg (Philadelphia: Fortress Press; Atlanta: Scholars Press, 1986), 223–37. See also S. P. Brock, C. T. Fritsch, S. Jellicoe, eds., *A Classified Bibliography of the Septuagint* (Leiden: E. J. Brill, 1973). D. W. Gooding, "A Sketch of Current Septuagint Studies," in *Proceedings of the Irish Biblical Association* 5 (1981): 1–13, offers a good survey of the issues. For current literature, see *Elenchus: Die international Zeitschrift für Bibelwissenschaft* and the *Bulletin of the International Organization for Septuagint and Cognate Studies.* See also the Congress volume in *Supplements to Vetus Testamentum*, ed. J. A. Emerton, vol. LX (Leiden: E. J. Brill, 1988); and Klaus Berger, *Die Gesetzauslegung Jesu: Ihr historischer Hintergrund im Judentum und um Alten Testament*, vol. 1, *Markus und Parallelen* (Neukirchen-Vluyn: Neukirchener Verlag, 1972), esp. 100–36, 137–47, and 258–77. Also of value are Peter Katz, *Philo's Bible: The Aberrant Text of Bible Quotations in Some Philonic Writings* (Cambridge: Cambridge University Press, 1950) and Sidney Jellicoe, *The Septuagint and Modern Study* (Oxford: Oxford University Press, 1968). More recently, see Schürer, *History of the Jewish People,* 474–93; and Marguerite Harl, et al., *La Bible Grecque des Septante, du Judaisme Hellénistique au Christianisme Ancien* (Paris: Éditions du Cerf, 1988).

7. J. A. L. Lee, *A Lexical Study of the Septuagint Version of the Pentateuch* (Chico, Calif.: Scholars Press, 1983), has proven that the Greek of the Septuagint was the Greek of the time. The translation process caused the peculiarities found there. This same view is shared in Marguerite Harl, ed., *La Bible d'Alexandrie: La Genese* (Paris: Éditions du Cerf, 1986), who argues in the preface that the Greek of the LXX was not a Jewish-Greek dialect but the ordinary language of the time, which despite its Hebraisms was fully intelligible.

8. Georg Bertram, "Das Problem der Umschrift und die religionsgeschichtliche Erforschung der Septuaginta," *BZAW* 66 (1936): 109, states, "Die Septuaginta gehört mehr in die Geschichte der Auslegung des Alten Testaments als in des alttestamentlichen Textes." Bertram's statement may be a bit extreme, but it is valid, nevertheless, in some sense.

9. Notable exceptions, however, do exist. See I. L. Seeligmann, *The Septuagint Version of Isaiah: A Discussion of Its Problems* (Leiden: E. J. Brill, 1948); Georg Rosen, *Judem und Phoenizier: Das jüdischen Diaspora*, rev. Friedrich Rosen and D. Georg Bertram (Tübingen: J. C. B. Mohr, 1929); G. Bertram, "Zur Bedeutung der Religion der Septuaginta in der hellenistischen Welt," *TLZ* 92 (1967), 245–50;

G. Bertram, "Vom Wesen der Septuaginta-Frömmigkeit," in *Die Welt des Orients* 3 (1956): 274–84; John W. Olley, *Righteousness in the Septuagint of Isaiah: A Contextual Study* (Missoula, Mont.: Scholars Press, 1978); H. M. Erwin, "Theological Aspects of the LXX of the Book of Psalms" (unpublished diss., Princeton Seminary, 1962).

10. After the work of Dietrich-Alexander Koch, *Die Schrift als Zeuge des Evangeliums, untersuchung zur Verwendung und zum Verständnis der Schrift bei Paulus* (Tübingen: J. C. B. Mohr, 1986) there should be little doubt that the Septuagint was the Bible of Paul. Over half a century ago Adolf Diessmann, *Paulus* (Tübingen: J. C. B. Mohr, 1925), 69, anticipated Koch with his description of Paul as a Septuagint-Jew.

11. Henry Barclay Swete, *Introduction to the Old Testament in Greek* (Cambridge: Cambridge University Press, 1934), 1:314.

12. Seeligmann, *Septuagint Version of Isaiah,* 106.

13. See Martin Flashar, "Exegetische Studien zum Septuaginta-Psalter," *ZAW* 32 (1912): 161–89, especially 169–70.

14. See 24:20; 43:25; 44:22; 53:5; 59:12a; and 59:12b.

15. See 6:7; 27:9; 50:1; 59:3; and 64:5.

16. See 55:7b and 58:1.

17. See 59:4 and 59:6.

18. Victor Tcherikover, "The Ideology of the Letter of Aristeas," *HTR* 51 (1958): 77–79.

19. See Tcherikover, "Ideology," 65.

20. Ibid., 63.

21. In *Hellenistic Civilization and the Jews* (New York: Atheneum, 1970), 128–72, Tcherikover correctly notes that laws and customs taken for granted and therefore unchallenged needed no defense. Only those in danger of rejection by Jews as irrational prescriptions needed and received a rational defense by Pseudo-Aristeas. See also "Ideology," 60–63.

22. See Schürer, *History of the Jewish People,* III, 140–41.

23. See Tcherikover, "Ideology," 57–85.

24. Leon Festinger, *When Prophecy Fails* (Minneapolis: University of Minnesota Press, 1956), suggested as much in showing how the attempt to win converts compensated in Lake City, Minnesota, for a disconfirmation crisis when the end predicted failed to occur.

25. Tcherikover, "Ideology," 83.

26. Ibid.

27. J. J. Collins, *Between Athens and Jerusalem: Jewish Identity and the Hellenistic Diaspora* (New York: Crossroad, 1983), 86.

28. For example, he extols moderation that brings health (237, 245), restrains anger (253), promotes self-discipline (211, 221), and enhances self-esteem (223–24). He stresses piety, love of humanity, generosity, magnanimity, prudence, justice, and temperance—all Hellenistic traits of the ideal Hellenistic man, or *kalokagathos.*

29. One might argue that *kosmopolitou* here is hardly a universalistic term but rather a term with a sharp vertical dimension and has little direct relevance for this discussion. But its association with the creation of the world would seem to gainsay that position.

30. For example, Themistocles' daughter married her brother (Plutarch, *Them.* 32).

31. Perhaps following the example of the marriage of Isis and Osiris.

32. Unfortunately, few deviants are allowed to speak for themselves, so we do not know if they intended to abandon Judaism. Certainly the boundary beyond

which one became an apostate is unmarked. Denial of the God of Israel, or initiation into one of the mysteries (319) would make one an apostate, but would loyalty to the Roman imperial administration make one an apostate? What had Philo's nephew, Tiberius Alexander, done to earn the condemnation Philo heaped on him?

33. S. J. D. Cohen, "Crossing the Boundary and Becoming a Jew," *HTR* 82 (1989): 13–33, argues that "in Alexandria in the first century, the tension between the Jews and the gentiles was so great that virtually no gentiles became adherents or proselytes" (32–33). Philo's repeated defenses of the rights of the proselytes do suggest tensions existed, but Cohen goes too far with his claim that proselytism essentially ceased.

34. Schürer, *History of the Jewish People,* III, 140, correctly notes the tendency in the Diaspora community to emphasize general religious ideas such as the idea of the supreme God to harmonize Jewish and Greek culture, and the emphasis on the universal elements evoked tolerance from the Greek environment. Proselytism, as Vermes and others maintain, may itself have brought about a tendency toward an attenuated Judaism.

35. Tcherikover, "Ideology," 81.

36. See R. J. Z. Werblowsky, "Paulus in jüdischer Sicht," in *Paulus-Apostat oder Apostel,* ed. M. Barth et al. (Regensburg: Kluwer, 1977), 135-46, esp. 139.

37. Nils Dahl, "The One God of Jews and Gentiles (Romans 3:29–30)," in *Studies in Paul* (Minneapolis: Augsburg, 1977), 190.

38. Ibid.

39. One might agree with Mussner, however, that *pas* is the key word for understanding Romans (F. Mussner, "Heil für Alle," *Kairos* 23 [1981]: 207–14). But to emphasize inclusion with no sense of its history in the Diaspora is to miss important dimensions of its development and application. I agree with Lloyd Gaston that his inclusion "must not be interpreted in a disinterested, even-handed, universalizing theological manner." See L. Gaston, *Paul and the Torah* (Vancouver: University of British Columbia Press, 1987), 126–34. But I might be more attentive to the universalizing tendencies of Diaspora Judaism than is Gaston.

40. See Mussner, "Heil für Alle."

41. See Lloyd Gaston, "For *All* the Believers: The Inclusion of Gentiles as the Ultimate Goal of Torah in Romans," in *Paul and the Torah* (Vancouver: University of British Columbia Press, 1987), 116–34.

42. See Arnold van Gennep, *The Rites of Passage* (London: Routledge, 1960; French ed., 1909).

43. See Victor Turner, *The Ritual Process: Structure and Anti-Structure* (Ithaca, N.Y.: Cornell University Press, 1969). This tendency, however, according to Turner, is not limited to ritual. See his "Myth and Symbol," in the *International Encyclopedia of Social Sciences,* ed. David L. Sills (New York: Macmillan and the Free Press, 1968), 10:576–79.

44. The position of W. Gutbrot that "In Judaism *ho anomos* or *hoi anomoi* is a common term for the Gentiles" (*TDNT,* 4:1087), while generally correct, ignores the ambiguities created by Gentiles living on the boundary of Judaism, and misses the tension let loose in the Diaspora Jewish community by its interaction with the dominant culture. Once one sees the Hellenistic culture as a lively cohort in active conversations with the Jewish community, the neat distinctions become less useful.

45. Dahl, "One God of Jews and Gentiles," 190.

Chapter 6

1. *Oxford English Dictionary,* 2d ed. (Oxford: Oxford University Press, 1989), 6:743.
2. For example, see the recent work of D. Z. Phillips, *Faith after Foundationalism* (London: Routledge, 1988). Especially germane are his discussions of "Grammar and Theology" (195–254) and "Manners without Grammar" (131–94). Important for this discussion is George A. Lindbeck, *The Nature of Doctrine: Religion and Theology in a Postliberal Age* (Philadelphia: Westminster, 1984), 79–84; and Wayne Proudfoot, *Religious Experience* (Berkeley: University of California Press, 1985). See also Paul Holmer, *The Grammar of Faith* (New York: Harper & Row, 1978).
3. Ludwig Wittgenstein, *Philosophical Investigations,* trans. G. E. M. Anscombe (New York: Macmillan, 1968), 116. G. P. Baker and P. M. S. Hacker have a very useful discussion of grammar in Wittgenstein in their *Wittgenstein, Rules, Grammar, and Necessity* (Oxford: Basil Blackwell, 1985), 34–80.
4. Lindbeck, *Nature of Doctrine,* 79–84.
5. Ibid., 114. I am aware of the substantive criticism of Lindbeck offered by D. Z. Phillips *(Faith after Foundationalism,* 196–225); however, Phillips agrees with Lindbeck's critique of foundationalism in theology.
6. My own study of the *theodidaktoi* inclines me in that direction. See my *"Theodidaktoi* and Handwork in Philo and 1 Thessalonians," in *L'apôtre Paul: Personnalité, style et conception du ministère,* ed. A. Vanhoye (Louvain: Leuven University Press, 1986), 324–31.
7. I use the term "elite" here in the French sense of *d'elite* meaning "choice, pick, or select."
8. Even allowing for the presence of other concerns in the letter (e.g., 4:1–9), Karl Donfried's view that this letter is primarily a response to persecution deserves further discussion. His ideas are developed in "The Theology of 1 Thessalonians as a Reflection of Its Purpose" (a paper distributed to members of the "Consultation on the Theology of Paul" at the annual meeting of the Society of Biblical Literature in 1986).
9. The absence of subversive discourse and the presence of so much teaching, encouragement, reminding, and exhortation led Abraham Malherbe to call this a parenetic letter. Although he has argued this in many places, see his *Paul and the Thessalonians: The Philosophic Tradition of Pastoral Care* (Philadelphia: Fortress Press, 1987).
10. Note the same association in *1 Enoch* 100:5; CD (Damascus Document) 4:4–6; and Dan. 7:18, 22, 25, and 27. Donfried also notes the distinctive but not unique character of the holiness language in 1 Thessalonians and links it with persecution in Jewish martyrological literature ("Theology of 1 Thessalonians," 5–6).
11. I understand Paul to use "the upward calling of God" in 3:14 not as a synonym of his election, that is, call into Christ, but as an expression of his elect status.
12. For this insight I am indebted to Ralph Martin, *Carmen Christi: Philippians ii. 5–11 in Recent Interpretation and in the Setting of Early Christian Worship,* SNTSMS 4 (Cambridge: Cambridge University Press, 1967).
13. Of course, the identity of these circumcisers and their provenance is hotly disputed. All of the possibilities have been carefully outlined by Hans Dieter Betz *(Galatians: A Commentary on Paul's Letter to the Churches in Galatia,* Hermeneia [Philadelphia: Fortress Press, 1979]). While that discussion is terribly important, the question of whether the circumcisers were local Gentiles or emissaries from Jerusalem will have to be passed over for the moment.

14. Betz, *Galatians,* 263.

15. I am uncertain if "freedom" (*eleuthēria*) and "new creation" (*ktisis*) are cotermi-
    nous, as David Lull has suggested, but they are certainly complementary. Both
    clearly serve as descriptions of some aspect of the state of the believers. See David
    J. Lull, *The Spirit in Galatia: Paul's Interpretation of Pneuma as Divine Power,*
    SBLDS 49, (Chico, Calif.: Scholars Press, 1978), 110.

16. On this point I agree with Heinrich Schlier, *Der Brief an die Galater,* 5th ed. (Göt-
    tingen: Vandenhoeck & Ruprecht, 1971), 242–43, against Betz, *Galatians,*
    272–73. Having grown up in a Diaspora community, Paul could hardly have
    been unaware of these charges brought against Jews who drifted too close to or
    beyond the boundary.

17. Instead of "Every man hanged from a tree is cursed by God" (LXX), Paul has,
    "Cursed be everyone who hangs on a tree" (LXX). Paul removes the reference to
    God ("cursed by God" in the LXX). Paul's change suggests that he was unwilling
    to say Jesus' crucifixion was due to God's curse.

18. A voluminous secondary literature discusses the identity of Paul's addressee in
    this passage. The best summaries of contrary views are by Betz *(Galatians,*
    322–23} and Peter Richardson (*Israel in the Apostolic Church* [Cambridge: Cam-
    bridge University Press, 1969], 79–84). Betz makes a strong case for reading this
    passage in its most restrictive and abrasive sense, namely, to apply only to believ-
    ers in Christ. He notes precedents for such a reading in the Qumran literature.
    Richardson solves the problem in the passage by punctuating the sentence as fol-
    lows: "May God give peace to all who will walk according to this criterion, and
    mercy also to his faithful people Israel."

19. On this point I agree with Beverly Gaventa, "The Singularity of the Gospel: A
    Reading of Galatians," in *Pauline Theology I* (Minneapolis: Fortress Press, 1991),
    147–59.

20. While deconstructionism ignores broad reconstructionist tendencies in Paul's
    theology, the warning of J. Hillis Miller is apt: "Deconstruction attempts to resist
    the totalizing and totalitarian tendencies of criticism. It attempts to resist its own
    tendencies to come to rest in some sense of mastery over the work" ("The Critic
    as Host," in *Deconstruction and Criticism,* ed. H. Bloom et al. [New York: Seabury
    Press, 1979], 252).

21. I am aware of William Baird's recent article "'One against the Other': Intra-
    Church Conflicts in 1 Corinthians," in *The Conversation Continues: Studies in
    Paul and John in Honor of J. Louis Martyn,* ed. Robert T. Fortna and Beverly R.
    Gaventa (Nashville: Abingdon Press, 1990), 116–36. I am in sympathy with his
    basic point, but the considerations here do not require that fine distinctions
    between groups be drawn.

22. This inversion resembles William Buckley's famous comment about the conser-
    vatives' reliance on the *New York Times.* Conservatives, he noted, read the *Times*
    and then simply think the opposite.

23. See S. Scott Bartchy, ΜΑΛΛΟΝ ΧΡΗΣΑΙ: *First-century Slavery and the Inter-
    pretation of 1 Corinthians 7:21,* SBLDS 11 (Missoula, Mont.: Scholars Press,
    1973).

24. John C. Hurd, *The Origin of 1 Corinthians* (London: SPCK, 1965), 158–62. The
    emphasis on spiritual marriages (7:5), celibacy (7:7), and separation from unbe-
    lievers (7:12–16) all point in the direction of some form of asceticism as the dis-
    tinguishing mark of the elect.

25. Bartchy, ΜΑΛΛΟΝ ΧΡΗΣΑΙ: *First-century Slavery,* 152.

26. See my *Paul: The Man and the Myth* (Minneapolis: Fortress Press, 1997), 127–31.

27. Helmut Koester, "Historic Mistakes Haunt the Relationship of Christianity and Judaism," *Biblical Archaeology Review* 21 (March-April 1995): 26–27.
28. Terence L. Donaldson, *Paul and the Gentiles: Remapping the Apostle's Convictional World* (Minneapolis: Fortress Press, 1997), 299.
29. Ibid.
30. For a fuller discussion of this issue see my "Jewish Christian–Gentile Christian Relations: A Discussion of Ephesians 2:15a," *ZNW* 74 (1983): 81–89.
31. On this point I agree with Donaldson, *Paul and the Gentiles,* 297–98.

Index of Ancient Sources

Index of Subjects and Authors